W9-AUR-464

GEMMA BOVERY

by the same author

MRS WEBER'S DIARY
TRUE LOVE
PICK OF POSY
VERY POSY
PURE POSY
MUSTN'T GRUMBLE

for children

FRED
LULU AND THE FLYING BABIES
THE CHOCOLATE WEDDING
BOUNCING BUFFALO
F-FREEZING ABC

GEMMA BOVERY

Posy Simmonds

PANTHEON BOOKS
NEW YORK

Published in the United States by Pantheon Books, a division of Random House, Inc., New York. Originally published in book form in Great Britain by Jonathan Cape, London, in 1999.

Originally published in cartoon strip form in *The Guardian*.

Library of Congress Cataloging-in-Publication Data
Simmonds, Posy.
p. cm.
Originally published: London: J. Cape, 1999.
ISBN 0-375-42339-7
I. Title.
PN6737.S46G46 2005 741.5'942--dc22 2004053421

www.pantheonbooks.com
Printed in Mexico
First American Edition
2 4 6 8 9 7 5 3 1

FOR RICHARD

Normandy

The Present Day

Normandy 1998

Gemma Bovery has been in the ground three weeks. People have begun to forget – or anyway I don't hear talk in the shop any more. But I – I never stop thinking of her. The nights are worst. If I sleep, I dream of her dead eyes which are the blue of stained glass.

PAIN MAISON
JE PETRIS ET JE CUIS MON PAIN AU FOURNIL
Pain de Campagne
PAIN COMPLET

My name is Raymond Joubert. I have done several things in life, but for the past seven years I've been content to run the family bakery here in Bailleville. I am a Norman, the son of a baker. In spite of my sojournings abroad, my writing, my interest in the history of communications, I think I remain a simple man.

What I am now compelled to write – of the recent tragedy in our small town – is no more than an attempt to make some sense of what happened: an attempt to discover the facts and thereby the extent (or the limit) of my own culpability. Because – and this is difficult – in all this sorry business, I do not know how much to blame myself. My head tells me I am merely at fault, but my guts condemn me. How I suffer – my colonic agony, it's not just *à cause d'une colite*. I feel myself profoundly guilty.

However, I do not examine these events to soothe my digestion. I do it for my conscience, for the sake of my sanity.

Of course, now, I think something terrible will happen to Charlie Bovery. Everything else has. Why not his death? Of a broken heart is unlikely. He is English after all. But he'll do it with drink, or gas himself. Or crash his van.
I dread going to see him. But I feel I have to. I can't telephone, because theirs is cut off. *Pauvre salaud.* He's always there, half pissed. He mumbles in English.

Gemma
: uhh :
O bugger...
O Gemma!
: uhh :

But sometimes he says in French, and I find it unbearable:

Oh Raymond... vous êtes mon seul ami... vous êtes un vrai ami...

I have to be frank, when Charlie Bovery calls me his friend, I feel a shameful relief. It means he doesn't know of... certain things concerning me and his wife. He doesn't know that it was I, I who tempted the fates. I who lit the long fuse that led to that young woman's death.

The blood of Gemma Bovery is on my hands. Up to a point.

Today, when I go round to see poor Bovery he's in the kitchen, which has become very foul since Gemma died. The house is up for sale, but no one'll want it, stinking like that.
As usual, Charlie's doing crosswords in the papers the other local English save for him. He's no good at them, but always takes a childish pride in solving anagrams.

GIANT MICE, Raymond...
...how amazing!

Des souris? Yes. You 'ave mice
No! It's an anagram... ...see...of ENIGMATIC

And look, see..BEDROOM ...it makes BOREDOM...

I'm thinking, Ah, BEDROOM/BOREDOM, very fitting for the prudish *anglais*. Then I see Charlie looking up to where he and Gemma slept overhead. It's a horrible moment, because one supposes there must have been boredom in that bedroom . . . because of what happened. Even more embarrassing, his eyes are now full of tears.

Oh god, Raymond!

It's THESE, Raymond ...I found these..

They're hers. Gemma's. ...they're her diaries ...SIGH
!

M*erde*. I should have realised there'd be diaries. I forget young women keep diaries. And so many. Thin school exercise books. I feel almost nauseous, because it must all be in there, about her and me. I hardly dare meet Charlie's eyes, to see if he's read them, but he says "I can't read them, Raymond, I can't, not yet."

My instinct is to tell him to burn them at once. But curiosity writhes in me, like snakes in a pit. I need to know what she's written! I need to know so many things.

I have three or four drinks out of politesse. Then I do something despicable. Before I leave, while Charlie fumbles at the door, I slide the top diary off the pile into my coat. Hoping to God that it's the most recent, the most incriminating.

Allez, Charlie..ça va mieux maintenant, n'est ce pas? Bon, repose-toi...on se voir demain... au revoir!

I run back to my place, Gemma's diary burning in my armpit. I tell myself, I'm not a thief. I borrowed it to discover the facts – although why I expect to find facts in her diary, I don't know. The writing of the dead acquires strange authority. If Gemma were alive I'd read her version of events with suspicion.

I find an English dictionary amongst the mess in my son's room. Then I shut myself in my study.*
With intense nervosity I open Gemma's diary and suffer two disappointments: only six pages are written; it's not the one I was after! It's earlier, when she'd been in Normandy only a few months. But, tucked in the back, I discover something *vital*: the folded page of an English magazine also dated the same year.

* Yes, I have a study.
Although these days my time is taken up with the bakery, I'm still an associate editor of the quarterly review *Conjonctures* and contribute the occasional article.

Merde alors! c'est lui...
..Patrick Large!

Patrick Large! Her lover. So she knew him back then. Or perhaps before then, before I ever knew her. This means everything to me. It means she and he had a history. It means he didn't spring from nowhere...

With the help of my son's school dictionary I translate the article. It's some *saloperie* about Patrick's apartment in London. Plus two things I never knew.
He has a wife (Pandora)! And a child! Ha! So he's an adulterer too.

Across one of the photos there's a word scrawled in pencil, perhaps in Gemma's hand: WANKERS....

..wand...wane..wangle...
..want... merde, ce n'est pas là...
DICTIONNAIRE
ANGLAIS

I can't help feeling like the most base voyeur, as sentence by sentence I translate the six pages of diary. It's hard work. I don't stop even when I hear my wife return from the shop – it's normal for me to be at my desk at this hour and she knows not to disturb me. Also I am confident that Martine knows nothing of my involvement with Gemma or my recent chagrin. She thinks it's my irritable bowel that keeps me awake at night.

BAILLEVILLE

The first entry in Gemma's diary confirms something I already guessed. After only a few months of living in France she hates it. She hates Normandy. She hates Bailleville. She hates the rain.

Above all, the house is a profound disappointment.

The English have a great talent for cottaging and Gemma was no exception. She tried to recreate the atmosphere of a hundred years ago, as if peasants still lived there. (One would say very bourgeois peasants, owners of kelim rugs, butler's trays and English arm-chairs.) But I can imagine her depression . . . those small dark rooms, darker and smaller when her husband is in them.

Wherever Charlie is, he blocks the light. The rain falls, the muslin droops round the windows. All her possessions seem to retire into the shadows to die. The beams are gibbets of lynched, dangling things.

And the deathly quiet. It ennerves her. She writes:

God, this bloody place!
It's like a morgue
NOTHING happens!
God I hate my life

At night she listens to Charlie snoring beside her. And begins to hate him too.

Several times in this diary Gemma mentions her insomnia.

I imagine her lying there counting her mistakes. Three bad choices: wrong husband, wrong house, wrong place.

Of course she no longer wants to have a child with Charlie. The image which used to entrance her in London – of blossom-scented air and tiny clothes drying in the orchard – is now appalling. She would die of boredom buried in Normandy, and so would the baby, when it grew. She knows this from her stepchildren's visits – Charlie's kids. Their holidays are her constant dread.

She writes a lot about Charlie. He looks a mess. He's clumsy, insensitive, distant. She can't talk to him. He bores her.

I would agree with the first charge. Charlie is not *soigné*. He's quite smelly, of tobacco, and the glue and varnishes he works with. His old sports shoes break every rule of hygiene.

But clumsy? I have seen him polishing in his workshop. He becomes almost graceful, his hand sweeping and looping over the surfaces. But perhaps he only loves wood. Perhaps he never caressed Gemma like that. Perhaps he never held her in the tender way he holds a Louis XVI *bergère*.

Poor Charlie! She wrote awful things about him. Things he should never read. Even then she was planning to leave him.

If only she had!

She would have spared herself, spared all of us, terrible anguish.

As I turn the page of the diary, everywhere Patrick Large's name leaps out at me. And it's quite clear. He and Gemma were lovers before she came to France. And she still loves him. Or rather, two years after their liaison, he still makes her smoulder at night, which comes to the same thing.

unh... Patrick...
.. bastard!..

I run my eye over the two final pages of Gemma's diary. My name isn't there. I feel relief and, perversely, a little insulted. Then I set about translating.

It's disgusting, and if I find it disgusting, God help Charlie Bovery if he ever reads it. But perhaps he knows, perhaps he's always been a complaisant husband. Perhaps he knew his wife lay beside him and fantasised about her ex-lover. It's an image I find quite erotic – much more erotic than her fantasy, which is banal stuff about going back to London – meeting Patrick, him falling in love with her again because she's got impossibly thin and beautiful. *Pouah*! It's the worst kind of cinema.

What's the matter, Patrick? You're not eating... Isn't it good?
Uh! It's YOU, Gemma ..you're SO beautiful!
Let's just skip lunch, yeah?
Uhh! I'm crazy for you Gemma!
What about your deadline, Patrick?
Sod the deadline!
Unh! Gemma.. God! I LOVE you!
Unh unh! Gemma! Oh, Gemma!
What is it, Gemma?
You OK?
It's that pâté, isn't it? Was so rich... I've got a helluva gut-ache, too
Uhh
Uh

Most days I lunch at home with my wife. Afterwards Martine returns to the shop and I take a nap on the sofa. I'm always exhausted – up at five preparing the dough with Jean and André and baking all morning.
I don't do the afternoon shift any more. I'm feeling my age. Today I feel a thousand.

But I don't sleep. I think of Gemma's diary in my desk drawer and whether I have the moral right to destroy it. Bovery really shouldn't read it. Then I think of those other diaries lying in his kitchen and decide it would be doing both of us a service if I borrowed them too, and if I censored – tore out – the painful bits.
From the sofa I can see across the field to Charlie's house. I can't look in that direction now without thinking of him the day Gemma died. Their telephone had been cut off and he came rushing over to use ours. I can't forget his face – his bleeding nose. The bleeding nose troubles me. He never said anything then or later how he got it. Never mentioned it. When the *pompiers* came he'd mopped himself up. It's occurred to me since that Martine and I were the only ones to see it. And his glasses were broken. Was there a fight? Did Gemma hit him, or what?
I have a bad feeling about it.

Joubert! She's dead! She's DEAD!

Oh God! Oh God! Oh God...
ALPHA ROUEN

I have a bad feeling about Charlie, generally.
It's crazy, but I think his life is still in the grip of some malign force. I despise superstition, yet every day I dread news of his sudden death. I feel it in my guts (the *rillettes de porc*, perhaps. Or maybe Dutronc is right, I should give up wine.) But I reassure myself, there are solid rational grounds for morbid speculation. Charlie Bovery has every reason to be suicidal: his wife's death, financial trouble, Gemma's debts – his debts. I've heard about those.
The *English* tax people are really after him.

!

I smell burning.
Across the field Bovery's house is obscured by smoke. Of course, I think he's set light to himself and the house. It's happening.
Pauvre crétin. He's ending it all.
And then a worse thought strikes me: he's read Gemma's diaries. Now he's burning them and I shall never know what's in them.

I discover Charlie burning some of his wife's effects, things which blaze and fizzle to nothing.

Gemma's underwear. First, a heap of chaste, ample things, a little dingy. Veterans, I suppose, of the time she was fat.

And then there's the other stuff: every sort of vile female packaging she wore, not out of self-love, but as a submission to the diktats of the sexual marketplace. I recognise the red *soutien-gorge* with the vicious under-wiring and the lace basque which forced that deep breathless cleft.

Burning's too good for it all. I feel a terrible anger – anger at Gemma, resorting to these pernicious trussings, anger at the stupid waste of her life, anger at Charlie, the willing cuckold, and anger at the tightening I feel in my throat. (Guilt. Remorse!) "*You* let it happen, Charlie", I think, as I watch him, the poor dolorous widower, feeding the pyre. "You're guilty too. Admit. Confess!"

uUh...Joubert..Raymond!
oh God, the smoke...You O.K?

Sorry! Excusez-moi... You OK? Just thought it better to burn this... didn't want the dustmen to... You OK?
ouioui c'est rien

Come inside...have a drink ...I need one
sank you

I feel better in the kitchen. Better from the Scotch. Better because Gemma's diaries are there and not burned, as I feared. (Before I go, I shall sneak a couple of them inside my shirt.) Also, as if in answer to my silent entreaty, it's apparent that Charlie is ready to unburden himself.

Hunh I'll never get over her, Raymond...Never.. Hunhh ..it's the bad stuff...there's really bad stuff... Huuhh ...can't handle it...

Charlie.....eezaire somesing about your wife's death you weesh to tell me?

I was bold enough to ask Charlie where he first met Gemma. He said it was at a party in London one Christmas Eve. Gemma was standing alone holding an unopened champagne bottle, looking distraught.

Bastard!
bastard
bastar!!

Um..shall I open that for you?

THIS is the way to open champagne..
NOT with a bang..
..but with the SIGH of a contented woman...

You're not contented, are you?

"She began to cry," Charlie said, "It was awful."
"Why did she cry?" I asked. Charlie buried his head in his hands, and I was worried he wouldn't tell me anything else. But after a minute Charlie said Gemma was depressed because she had flu and because she hated the time of year.

!

Her mother had died at Christmas when she was a child. And she was on her own that Christmas. She couldn't face going to her father's in the country because she always had a row with her stepmother.

So Charlie took her home with him. "What else could I do?" he said, "She looked like death"... Although she was alive enough apparently to admire his van and his apartment in somewhere called Hackney.

Wow! Split-screen V.W!! Hey, great!!

Ooh...nice cornice ...early Georgian, yeah?

Great flat... is it yours?
No..rented

God!
Amazing chair

Not mine..it's a client's ...I've got to do a bit of work on it...
Is that what you do?

Yeah..that's what I do... I restore things.. .....

I asked Charlie what happened next day, Christmas Day. He said "Not much." Gemma was worse and he was supposed to be cooking turkey for his ex-wife and kids in another part of London. Then he fell silent. Who knows what he was remembering?

Got any Lem-sip... ..Neurofen.... ..Kleenex?
Only bog roll
rrrRing!
Judi! Happy Christmas!
Where the HELL are you!?
I'm sorry! I'm sorry! Look, I'll be round in an hour... I'll deal with the turkey then... leave EVERYTHING to me... I'll...
The kids are SO disappointed! ...you SAID you'd be here for breakfast!
I KNOW! I'm SORRY! ..but I've got to go and find a chemist's
God, Charlie, you're such a bloody hypochondriac!
Not ME..someone else ...they're really ill...
Who? WHO's ill?
Um..a girl...
D'you mean a girl or a woman? Don't call women girls, Charlie!
Woman, then ..well, she's younger than us...
Yes, she would be, wouldn't she, Charlie?
Just met, have you?
Judi! She's...
Charlie, your private life's YOUR business.. I don't want to hear any more..
...but in your place, I'd put my children FIRST on Christmas Day!
Charlie on his way, is he?
Dunno, Mum...first he's going to the chemist.... then he's giving some little tart breakfast in bed....

I didn't learn much more about that Christmas. Charlie said he and his ex-wife shared the child care in a civilized way – he went each day to the matrimonial home in Islington. His ex-wife's name is Judi (he averted his eyes when he said it.)

About **Bloody** time! You **KNEW** I was going out! I'm **LATE**! **Honestly**!..too busy playing doctors and nurses, that's your trouble... **bloody** well take Delia and go and fetch Justin from the Cardews!...and when you get back.. **DON'T** just shove them in front of the **telly**... **DO** something with them!
I'll be back tonight..about twelve thirty
Boots
Chips

Uh..not till then? I..er...I ought...

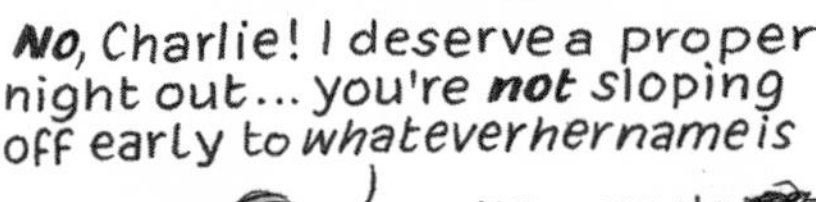
NO, Charlie! I deserve a proper night out... you're **not** sloping off early to *whateverhernameis*

Her name's Gemma

Oh. Gemma, is it?...Ah. Well, lucky **HER**! When I have flu, I have it standing up....

At night he would return to his flat to nurse Gemma – *Cette inconnue – cette dame aux camélias.*

Beechams
LEMSIP
LEMSIP

I think it was then he fell in love with her (although it's hard to imagine his doing anything so unphlegmatic). But no, I'm maligning him. I know he loved her, and continued to love her in spite of everything, until the day she died. My question is, "did she ever love him?"

Gemma Bovery's diaries are hidden in my desk. There are twelve of them now. Stolen property. When I unlock the desk, I feel queasy, as if I'm breaking into her grave, as if her life is rotting in there and I'll touch something unspeakable.

But when I open the diaries (which are nothing more than school exercise books), I'm filled with a ravenous curiosity. At the sight of her nervous English script bolting over the page, I become like a pack of hounds in pursuit of a vixen.

I reach for the new, big dictionary I bought in Rouen.

I begin with the journal she wrote five years ago on New Year's Day. A frenzied scrawl. As I might have guessed, the cause of her anguish is Patrick Large. (I knew it!) On Christmas Eve around 2pm, she describes going past his flat, partly out of habit, partly out of suspicion. She sees first his car, then Patrick himself coming out of the building with a woman she recognises. She watches them snog (?), get in their cars, and drive away in opposite directions.

She wants to die. She has a fever, the beginning of flu. All the same she goes to the party that evening, where she encounters for the first time the gallant Charlie Bovery. And she weeps, not for the reasons Charlie told me, but because she'd been betrayed.

The rest I know – he nurses her for several days in his apartment. Whether anything else happened between them is not clear. I think not. Charlie's name appears only once or twice in this entry. She thinks he is "really kind". She worries what he overheard of a phone call she makes.

to snog...:
..se bécoter...
...hnm....
LE ROBERT & COLLINS
DICTIONNAIRE ANGLAIS
ANGLAIS

Yeah?
Uh..Patrick ...it's me
Gemma?? You sound funny...
I've got flu...
You poor baby... I was going to call you... You at your flat? Or still at your Dad's?
Didn't go to my Dad's
I'm at a friend's
God, Christmas is hell.... Just goes on and on... it's worse in the country... couldn't wait to get away.....
How was the shopping, Christmas Eve? Bet Stratford was disgusting...
******* nightmare!
Don't remind me!
I will remind you, Patrick!..... ...cos you weren't bloody there, were you!?
You were at your flat! I SAW YOU!... You and Pandora!
You bloody LIED!..gave me all that crap about having to leave early to go to your parents...!
Gemma, look...I don't keep tabs on you....
Anyway, I'm not talking about it...
Well don't, then! Just **** off! **** off! **** off!!!
Phew! WHO you telling to get double-dog-knotted? ....on my phone
Oh God, Charlie!

When she felt a little recovered from flu, Gemma left Charlie's and returned to her own apartment, in Shepherds Bush, the West 12 *arrondissement* of London.

And there, according to the diary, she stayed, suffering from a far more debilitating virus: LOVE . . . F***ing love, as Gemma referred to it, f***ing love, which made her blind enough to fall for f***ing Patrick. Who she loved as she never loved anyone before. Who dumped her. Therefore f*** love! She never ever wants a man to mean that much again.

And as for the force feeding! Seventeen pounds she's put on. Patrick stuffed her, fattened her like a pig and then left her for Pandora Kent (size 8).

The force feeding may be true. Patrick took her to thirty-five restaurants, a prodigious number, given the brief duration of the affair. But then of course, Patrick's *métier* was eating. He was food critic of *CitiZone*. (I assume that was how they met.
I know Gemma did illustrations for magazines amongst other things.)
Besides restaurants, Patrick took her to private clubs, private views, book launches, a tasting of British cheeses. She became part of a London milieu she now dismisses as full of posers and "tossers" (?). In the weeks of their liaison, she appeared in his reviews as "my companion", and in his bed he called her "sausage". ("Sausage." I nearly gag. *C'est affreux, ça. Ah, les anglais.*)

Name's LARGE...
table for two

Gemma calls Patrick other names in this diary and it warms my heart to read them: "Shit" (12 times) and many kinds of bastard: cold; cynical; lying; callous; patronising. He made her feel stupid. He name-dropped. He stared over her head at other women, he . . .
But the more I read, the more I ask myself, what did she see in this disgusting man? This man who regards himself in mirrors, who lectures her at table, who never asks her opinion (except about the food).

We'll all be barking, unless we start eating HORSEMEAT.... Why? I tell you...
Horses - they're so removed from our food chain, right? So, no common parasites, no...

MENU

What did she see in him, this man whose old reviews she reads over and over in her cold apartment?

I have to face the dreary and predictable answer – *C'était une bonne affaire au lit.*
He was good in bed.

Widgeons
2 Brinkley Street, London W1

Another below par restaurant which seeks to impress with its over-long menu,napkins likeblankets,Brobdingnagian wine glasses. The decor's red and overstuffed like the (mostly male) punters. The carpet pattern looks like a series of nose-bleeds. The food's a mess too. My pasta and woodland mushrooms had a whiff of marsh gas. My com-panion's lobster was a very nasty package – an overkill of coriander in the vinaigrette – and the cuttlefish-ink risotto was dried out. Sweetbreads and capers were OKish but they came, unaccountably, with a tumulus of flaccid chips. We gave the pud a miss. Two bottles of sumptuous (nicely over-oaked) Chardonnay were the sole excitements. Wine included, £120 for 2.

CiTiZONE
DKNY

I ask myself, do I want to read evidence that Patrick Large was a great lay? *Non!* But perhaps I want to read something positive if only to reassure myself that Gemma wasn't completely *masochiste*. However, she writes nothing favourable in this diary, which isn't surprising. The moment to recall his charms isn't now – the end of the affair is the time to remember other things, things of a more or less profound repugnance.
Such as (and I summarize):

RESTAURANTS
patrick large
WI

- The palm-wood salad servers Patrick gave her for Christmas.
- His by-line photo in *CitiZone*.
- The terrible illustrations she did for his page, particularly the lobster. During their affair she just couldn't draw. She never wants to work for *CitiZone* again.
- He throws books in the bin after reading them.
- The repulsive way he checks his breath before parties by going "huhhh" into his hands.
- His hatred of the Family (although she shares his theory that the adjective "family" degrades any noun it qualifies, e.g., meal, car, holiday.
- His anal tidiness. His clothes folded like Benetton; loose change in little pyramids; the fridge where he keeps coffee and Polaroid films.
- His apartment. Everything he owns is monochrome. Boring, clichéd, anonymous, lacking any risk or imagination.
- Only two of his possessions are redeemingly offensive.

1: an 85%-polyester duvet cover bought by his mother. It has maroon, pink and grey chevrons, an unpleasant feel, and often "a strong smell of comfort*".
2: a present from his sister, a silk tie with penguins "on the job*"
(*What? *Je n'ai aucune idée que veut dire ces usages.*)

It's the memory of the duvet cover which is absolutely the worst for Gemma. This duvet under which she has lain – at least thirty times – under which Patrick had whispered to her. (1: You're the first person I've ever wanted to be faithful to.
2: I think you're extraordinary.
3: You have the most wonderful tits.)
This duvet under which she'll never lie again, now covers the little cow, Pandora Kent.

Comfort
PRADA
MILANO
I give it three months
– it CAN'T last!! it just
can't last!
Patrick'll use her and then
dump her... or perhaps she'll
dump HIM. Hope she'll
give him a really hard time
Bastard! bastard bastard!

And it's agony! Agony. Everything about Pandora is *insupportable* – her bag, her tiny underwear, her smart background, her Cambridge degree, her ambition.
(She's already deputy editor of *CitiZone*.) She's chic, she's rich, she's invited everywhere, including now, Patrick Large's bed.

TATLER
HELLO!
VOGUE

Cocooned in her misery, Gemma hardly thought of Charlie Bovery, until the day she found him on her doorstep. He was nervous, uncertain he'd pressed the right bell. She says in her diary that she was reluctant to ask him in, because her apartment was freezing and on that particular day it stank of garlic sausage – sausage she was drawing for the food page of a Sunday newspaper.

Charlie's presence made her suddenly aware of how much she hated the place. She writes that it's now associated "with love sickness, crying, sitting about trying not to phone bloody Patrick, writing him letters I never post". Then there was her decor, which pre-dated the affair with Patrick: "Horrible! Total crap. I must have been mad." Charlie had remarked that it looked like a load of stuff dropped off the back of a hearse.

Oh, it's just stuff from junk shops.. I sort of liked the effect... I had a sort of Gothic phase..sort of Pre-Raphaelite-y...
Really **SICK** of it now... ***hate*** it.... **HATE** this place, Charlie....

Once she'd begun, Gemma writes, she couldn't stop. She told Charlie she was totally fed up with everything, not just the apartment. She was sick of deadlines, sick of working for stupid magazines and stupid advertising agencies who just wanted her to do the same boring old stuff. She was sick of churning it out, even though the money was good. There just had to be more to life than that. She wanted to do something else, to have a complete change, wind down, and move. But at the moment she couldn't quite get her head round where.

Well... if you want you can come and doss at my place...

Oh Wow! You did the distressing! God, Charlie, it's brilliant!..Sort of old palazzo! This house's got SUCH potential!
...Mornin', Mrs Archer... cold 'un, int it? Oh, morning, Bert - I was just telling Shula....
Pot Noodl

I look up Hackney in my map of London and realise the house was in that sad, workers' quarter near the city, reminiscent of Dickens and Gustave Doré, an area full of the rank odour of penury. "But," Gemma writes, it was "really buzzy and full of artists, a great deli down the road and a pub where you can play *boules* outside." It pleased her Charlie's house was a listed building, which was still waiting to be restored. The rent was cheap.Charlie had lived there since the failure of his marriage.

A few weeks later Gemma moved in with Charlie. His place sounds grim to me – two unheated floors of an old house – but Gemma describes it as "great." Between the floorboards there was, she claims, real eighteenth-century dust. In the kitchen cupboard there was "mouse shit and Pop Tarts", and where Charlie had steamed off old wall-paper the scabby plaster looked "really brilliant!"

Immediately, it seems from the diary, Gemma was stripping, repainting, graining-and-varnishing, unblocking fireplaces, staining floorboards, mixing colours and making hangings. Charlie's apartment, and creating a certain period atmosphere, became her passion: *Hogarthy, smoke-blackened, cosy-shabby, all sort of clay pipes and piss pots.*

Charlie himself became her passion too. She doesn't mention bed, so one must assume it met with her approval , as everything else about him did – his laid-back-ness, pride in his work, lack of materialism, the smell of French polish, the sawdust on his clothes, his fingernails with their black crescents of honest dirt.

Gemma liked everything about him except two things: the idea of his kids and the sound of his ex-wife, who telephoned at night about "updates on homework, headlice, bum-aching family stuff."

I now recall "family" is a word that fills Gemma with nausea.

I can see that it was quite a risky business moving in with a divorced man. So much depended on the relationship with his ex-wife. If he and she fought like tigers, one risked being bitten oneself. No wonder Gemma was anxious to know how Charlie and Judi Bovery got on.
"I think OK", Gemma writes in her diary. She still hadn't met either Judi or the children. But she monitored Charlie's demeanour before and after visiting his kids (as he did almost daily), and whenever Judi's name came up.

Charlie... was your divorce very messy?
Sorry?
was my what..?
Your divorce ...was it messy?
Mmn?..my divorce..messy? You mean blood on the walls?
Nuooh...wasn't messy ....in fact it was quite civilised...well, about as civilised as it could be
Was one of those quick jobs - two years' separation and that was it
So...who wanted to split up **FIRST**? You...or Judi?
Mn?
Mn..Judi I s'pose
Judi? Did she kick you out? Did she have someone else?
What?...no.ooo..she didn't meet John till much later..and he didn't last long...No, our split was sort of ...**MUTUAL**...
...a sort of mutual **DRIFTING APART** after Delia was born...not *much* fun at the time... ...but we get on **FINE** now...*absolutely* **FINE**...Judi's no problem at all....

So, as I, Joubert, understand it – after every encounter with Judi, Charlie displayed no signs of recent tension, nervosity, stress. On the contrary, he looked to Gemma as normal, *c'est à dire* "Relaxed, laid back, a bit absent-minded."
Thus it's reasonable to conclude that Charlie and Judi had a rare thing among *divorcés* – a civilized relationship.

Right, well..s'ppose you want to slope off home now....*One thing* before you go — the kids haven't stayed with **you** for **over** a *month*!...and don't think I don't know why not....

...because it's completely obvious...now this woman friend of yours is around, the children take a **very poor second place**! Don't they, Charlie?
Sorry?
What did you say?
You **HEARD**!
Oh, cut it out Charlie! God, you get on my tits!
Cut **WHAT** out?

Stop pretending!..pretending not to hear...pretending you're miles away...You do it **all** the time!
I don't!

You bloody **DO**!...it gives you time to think up *lies*, doesn't it?...time to cover up what you *really* feel...

Not that you ever **feel** anything much....
Bloody emotional cripple...

Before long Charlie's kids came to visit. It amazes me the trouble Gemma took before this first meeting – the main room dressed, the chimney swept, the candles lit around the hearth. Very Dickens. "Tiny Tim would have felt at home," Gemma writes. Afterwards she reported:

It went OK–Justin's nice Delia less so–made an awful fuss about candle wax in her hair.

One suspects the mother of Delia and Justin of having interrogated them when they got home covered in wax.

Have a good time, darlings?
Yeah

It'd been OK. Dad's girlfriend was OK. Quite fat. Quite old. She'd kissed them. She was really rich, took them in a taxi twice. The London Dungeon was OK. Dad's house was different, tidy, floppy curtains.
It was really dark. Smelt of birthdays from all the candles. They'd learnt to put them out with spit.They had to eat sitting down. It was boring, they couldn't watch telly.
The chocolate mousse was yummy. Had six eggs in it. There were two kinds of Häagen-Dazs at lunchtime. Dad and Gemma whispered a lot.

Three days later Judi Bovery delivered an envelope.

Lyre Grove, Tuesday.

Charlie

I'm writing, since you "couldn't make" Family Evening here last night. These evenings are so important for showing our shared commitment ot the kids. Their welfare should be your primary concern, which it plainly isn't at the moment. I am really worried about the following:

1. I thought we agreed - a careful and gradual introduction of a new partner into the children's lives. I think Delia is really upset to know someone she's hardly met is sharing your bed. Not clever of you. In my case, at least John was sensitive about that.
2. Lighted candles: Your place is dangerous enough already - you've never fixed the banister - the kids always risk breaking their necks, now you want to incinerate them too.
3. I know you can afford to give them treats, but chocolate mousse with so many uncooked eggs is madness. Do think! Salmonella!!! Also, Justin's weight problem isn't helped by stuffing him with ice cream. I try to give them fresh fruit, although it's tough on my budget.

In view of the above, esp. no.1, I'm asking you to see them round here for the time beiing. Please keep to the routine. Finally, mortgage/kids' money - When can I expect it ? I'm sick of having to ask for it every time, even sicker of asking you to pay it by standing order. If it's your way of humiliating me it's pathetic.

Judi

"A memo from the children's school," Charlie told Gemma, putting it in his pocket. "I'll shove it in the Family file."

Charlie's Workshop London E2

O God!

...she's going to start being a pain in the arse...
....start screwing things up between me and Gemma...

...mucking up my life...just can't leave me alone...Tsk!
...oh well... File and forget...

God, she's a pain...look at it all...
...dunno why I keep it...
Judi kids

am writing because it
you never listen!
well for you, but some of
the real world unlike
shrug off your responsi
you used to have princi
even had political con

May 2 '94

arlie
bout the cheapest &
shoes you could find!
hate spending money
in and Delia, don't you
shoes won't last her 5 mi
just meanness on your
notice you don't sti
so don't plead p
I know y
and

3

You had a proper teaching job but you threw it up - you backed out of it like you back out of everything - like you backed out of our marriage. "Anything for a quiet life" - that's your motto. When things get tough you never face them - you withdraw. You run away!

Yes, I know you resigned 'on principle' [Interesting that no one else in yr department did, or was it just you who was ground down by admin and student numbers?]

When are you going to look for a proper job? / Tarting up antiques for your brother's shop isn't [illegible] idea of one. You should be contact[ing] those people you know at the other art colleges.

Do you have any idea how m[uch] or how much the kids cos[t] I shouldn't have to ask forced to because you My job won't pay the - the extra has to

Yours

Judi

Jan 12th 93

Charlie
ridiculous spending so
of money on a child's
got into you !? I'm
stupid extravagance!
Trying to buy her affect
absolutely pathetic.
very well for you
don't have the
How you ca
the gall
An

July 16
Dear Charlie — I got your note
and since you're paid in cash
NO WAY of knowing you
didn't declare all of
misled the court
my maintenance
higher fi
If

Too right I didn't declare absolutely ALL my income...
..Every month she gets £600 ...all I get is a bollocking... Is this fair?
Bitch! Guilt merchant!! Cow!.....grinding rectal ache...!
Ring Ring!
WAX

Oh..hi Judi

Two things. One: If I don't have that cheque by the end of the day, I'm going to see my solicitor...

Two: When you pick them up from school, Justin goes straight to Karate...Delia's got a birthday party at the Pyms'...Thornhill Road... Pick him up at 5·15...pick her up at 6·30. He'll need feeding.... I'll be back at 8·00. While you're there, you can look at my washing machine..it's not r...

Yeah
O.K
Will do

When Gemma saw no more of Charlie's children beyond "a few brief hellos," and nothing of his ex-wife other than "one very small hello," her estimation of him really went up. He'd sensed she'd found his children boring, and before it became an issue he kept them out of her way, saw them on their home ground. He was so understanding! This arrangement meant that the apartment in Hackney became an entirely adult space, devoted to the simple but civilised living which Gemma now had time for. Embracing Charlie's frugal life style had freed her from the treadmill of earning.

She now worked "just enough." Her old life with its "stress, deadlines, diets, lipstick, mad spends in Harvey Nicks," she thought really sad. Soon the only links with this time were the magazines whose subscriptions she couldn't quite bring herself to cancel.

Charlie told me she had a mania for magazines which began in childhood with the ones in her father's waiting room.
It was a magazine which inspired one last spend before her credit cards entered a period of semi-dormancy. She bought two Lloyd Loom chairs, a rosewood pole fire screen, several "Bloomsbury throws" for the seating and a quantity of paint for doing "Charleston twiddles."

PAINTED DECOR
OMEGA

HOUSE
THE WORLD OF INTERIORS

How it pleased her, this shabby but perfect little world, where she and Charlie would sit of an evening having dined on "collar of bacon." Charlie with his crosswords and amusing anagrams (ETHICS / ITCHES, GROANS / ORGANS, CHARLES DICKENS / CHILDRENS CAKES.)
And Gemma, now fatter and less blonde, writing her journal: "I never thought I could be happy. But I am. I've got everything."
But a few entries later, something is missing: Charlie.

NF

Charlie who is always discreetly absenting himself to perform fatherly duties in Islington. There is something over-considerate about his air, something hangdog and blindly obedient about his exits. Far from ignoring his previous family, Gemma becomes irritatingly conscious of them every time he leaves the house.
Was it this pull of kinship, this commanding familial tug that made her want to strengthen her own ties with Charlie? This is the supposition I make when I read the question that Gemma put to Charlie one night, after the guests had gone.

Charlie...would you ever get married again?
God no...

I mean, *Sorry*? What did you say?

At the beginning of July Gemma writes in her diary: "Decided to get married!" In September the ceremony took place at the register office in her home town, Reading. Between these dates she writes very little. Nothing at all about the proposal. Did Charlie ask her? Did she ask him? Did it arise from a passionate moment? I rather doubt it.

"Decided to get married!" Apart from the *point d'exclamation* there is no other index of excitement. Her only concern is that the wedding should be "very quiet." Her father (but not her stepmother) objected. Mr Tate, retired from his dental practice, had time on his hands to organise "something proper."

Doesn't MATTER Charlie's divorced, Gemma!....
Big Day in your life! Come on, have a church blessing....
No, Dad, really..we..
Mi-chael! If she doesn't want it, she doesn't want it!

Gemma! What's happened? You used to LOVE weddings! Remember all those TATLERS in the waiting room?...you used to spend HOURS looking at all the society dos, didn't you?... You loved the posh ones ..all the trimmings!

Mr Patrick Large and Miss Pandora Kent

Fairacres
...for a fabulous day

We provide the perfect setting for your wedding

- Complimentary Function Suite
- Table floral arrangements
- Red carpet on arrival
- Use of silver cake stand & knife
- Personal management throughout the Big Day
- Champagne Breakfast served in your Honeymoon suite
- Complimentary engraved silver gift

It's clear that Gemma now despises such weddings. Apart from the "showing off," they remind her of her Patrick Large. During their relationship he was always "going off to smart things in crypts without ME!" This is not the experience of his new lover, Pandora.

Was it just the thought of Patrick which made Gemma want to make this defining moment in her life so discreet? I, Joubert, have three further suppositions: that it was Inertia, Fear of Disappointment, and third, Failure of Imagination. She writes that she "can't quite see Charlie in a morning suit." She can't "quite see" herself in the venue her father wants – the Occasions Room whose decor is "just wonderfully, wonderfully tacky." She thought that "the whole event could be brilliantly kitsch, but I just can't get my head around it."

After a while her father's persistence made her angry.

Look, our friends' daughter...SHE married a divorcé-she had the FULL WORKS! Nice blessing...Windsor Blue Rolls Royce...WONDERFUL reception at the Country Club...superb eats...everything SIT DOWN... evening disco, you name it!
But Dad, I SAID! we don't WANT a lot of... extravagance!
Honestly, they do things very well there, now...do a lovely FINGER BUFFET.... ...bridal room's got a double jacuzzi, y'know?

Look, STOP going on about the ruddy cost...
Dad, I don't WANT the sort of wedding You can afford!
Think I can't afford it!?
NO! FANCY saying that! She's got no feelings!!

The quiet wedding took place.

..ungrateful and cruel! There! I had to say it, Gemma, 'cos you really upset your father...and ME! You should be ashamed!

..so you wonder WHAT DO they teach them at school?
Exactly! It's not the DOGS' fault ...it's the blasted OWNERS'! I mean, our road gets TERRIBLE...

Gemma became a wife. And soon after a dog owner: a small dog with a fringe, a present from Charlie. (Ah, poor dog, it's the little bitch that I, Joubert – and my own dog – will come to know well.)
Gemma named it after some obscure English artist, and perhaps her happiest moments with Charlie were throwing sticks in London Fields after lunch at the pub .

Carrington! Here! Good dog!

Gemma had visitors, as the newly married do. First her father and stepmother who were most anxious to see the new home. Of course there was much head-shaking over the house in Hackney, its dilapidation, the lack of mortgage and consumer durables. The artful unostentation of the rooms was not admired, nor were the walls Gemma had painted "in the manner of Duncan Grant and Vanessa Bell."

Not a very nice area for CHILDREN is it, Gemma?... You'll have to think of that, you know...
You need some nets, Gemma...or d'you LIKE people looking in?
BLOOMSBURY

Judi came this afternoon – really ratty about some cheque Charlie hasn't sent her – which I found in the kitchen. She went on and on about how terrible Charlie is about money.. how he controls her, because she always has to ask him for it.. and would I persuade him to do it by standing order. Bloody nerve! Then she asked me what I felt about the extended family...

What d'you mean?
Well, you HAVE got one, you know.... Delia and Justin...
They've been waiting...for you to invite them here...
Oh God, I thought... I mean, I thought you and Charlie had it all sorted... he sees them at your place
Yes.. but they want to know YOU .. you're their stepmother now...
It's very important to them

But... I thought you thought HERE wasn't very...
Child-Friendly? ..no, it's not...
Charlie's never bothered about this place... but it doesn't take much....
Just a bit of organising ..get him to mend the banister...
Good, well that's settled then... I'll tell the kids you'd like them to come here,.. yes?

Justin and Delia Bovery began to stay with Gemma and Charlie: one night mid-week, alternate weekends, half the school holidays, plus three evenings a week, when Charlie saw them in their own home. This arrangement was Judi Bovery's "unilateral decision," and Gemma writes that Charlie took it "lying down."

In fact Charlie welcomed it. Although he often pointed out that PARENT was an anagram of ENTRAP, he was an enthusiastic father. He liked taking the children into the workshop, showing them how he did things. He just liked having them around. So much so that when Judi added to the duty roster, he made no objection at all.

Gemma writes:

They're here all the time! Third weekend running Judi's had one of her "emergencies". She does it just for the hell of screwing up our free time. She gets Delia to ring and that's it – Charlie's such a push-over. Pays her all that maintenance to do less & less. They have such a SICK relationship. Judi really is weird – she loves dumping the kids on us. Same time she HATES them being with ME. I can see it on her face. Jealous I'm trying to be Mummy. That's what her bloody notes are about – turn me into NANNY. Her little minion.

GEMMA
Please remember, school Monday: Justin's swimming things. Delia's shorts for PE
Dinner money (£5 each)
DELIA: She must be taken all the way up to the classrooom, not just dropped at the gate. Check she has her asthma inhaler. She must stay in when the air's bad.
Please, no candles (asthma)
Keep dust to minimum. Keep dog off her bed.
Remind Charlie not to smoke near her.
JUSTIN: "Stop'n Grow" for nailbiting. Please see he uses it. Please monitor TV watching. Ditto video games. No Mortal Combat 3 or Killer Strike.
Most important
Please, please, never let them go unaccompanied to the park again, or ANYWHERE London's so dangerous - particularly where you live.
Gratefully

Judi

I **know** it's only across the road... but Judi doesn't like them going on their **own**! **I'll** go with them... ...I don't mind...
Oh for God's sake!

What IS she afraid of?!! ...newsagent's going to abduct them...show them the **PORN** shelf...?
Honestly! She's **obsessed!**

...and she's made them obsessed.. ...Kids think the entire world's populated by **perverts** and **toxicara worms**...
I mean, they're **INDOORS** all the time...like **HOUSE ARREST**...
they never go out, except under escort...**it's sick!**
How're they ever going to learn to be independent...**How're** they going to learn about **LIFE**??

...scent in the urine. During oestrus, lions mate very frequently. The female squats to show she is receptive ...and the male will...

Did Gemma mind her stepchildren's visits? Did she warm to Justin and Delia?

We're all going dahn the Arse-nal! They're the boys that we adore... They're the boys in red and white.. ...they're ****ing dynamite... ...

JUSTIN: who spits like a footballer; whose breath smells of E-numbers; whose favourite epithet is "dickhead"; who loses the key to his mountain bike twice a week; who leaves behind him a trail of crumbs and cola.

DELIA: whose name, Charlie had been sad to discover, is an anagram of AILED. Delia who does indeed ail, who has asthma; who is jealous; who looks at Gemma out of the top of her eyes "as if she's going to head-butt me."

Justin and Delia, whose every activity either costs money or involves a car journey or needs batteries; Justin and Delia, who can recite the names of pizzas but not a single wild flower. Justin and Delia, who, Gemma writes, are used by their mother "as a means of controlling Charlie and buggering up our life."
Gemma had soon had enough of it.

God, what did you say to her?
Said I'm not her unpaid nanny and we're bloody well having this week-end to ourselves...

She gave me a right earful about female solidarity....

God, and all that bleating about her lack of freedom... If she wants freedom, she shouldn't've had kids...it's like giving yourself a ball and chain and complaining you can't run...

Anyway, what IS she talking about!? She dumps them on US most of the time....

I suppose she thinks as you haven't got kids, you can't underst...
O, shut up, Charlie! ..that's her line: "You wait till you have them, Gemma!"

...meaning: "I hope they give you a bloody hard time... and serve you bloody right!"
So much for female solidarity

Actually, Charlie... I've been thinking... I've just realised something really, really SERIOUS...which would affect...well, to do if we had a baby..... we can't afford to MOVE, can we?
Move? Why would we want to move?

Charlie! I'm not bringing a kid up in Hackney!! or anywhere near your bloody EX-WIFE!!

I want to MOVE!!! I'm sick of your kids here all the time...sick of Judi ruling our lives!! Sick of the way you let her!! I want to MOVE!!!

Gemma, Gemma, Gemma!! We can't move!...these days, spaces like this cost a fortune in rent..we'd never find another one so cheap... You've scaled your earnings right down...I've got Judi's mortgage – right now, we haven't any money......well, I've got a bit, stuck away, from when I'm paid in cash – but not enough! We can't MOVE!

I KNOW! I know! I know! God, I'm such a FOOL! I used to earn masses! Why did I stop?! Why did I pack it in?

sh*t..sh*t!..I chose bloody Quality of Life...now I've made myself POOR....

One almost hears the wail coming from Gemma's diary – an incantation of urban *désespoir*, of bourgeois blues. She woke up one morning and really noticed, as if for the first time:

- the air, "like breathing through an old sock."
- the street, "pissed-off people, dog shit, windscreen glass, fast-food filth."
- The alley, "needles, cans, condoms, gross old mattresses."
- The nights, "sirens, car alarms, kids tipping supermarket trolleys off the high rise, non-stop Heavy Metal, two doors down."
- Her doorstep with "a load of sick on it like a map of Australia."

FOR SALE

Gemma wants out. "Out, out, out!" Not in a year's time, when she'll have earned some money, but immediately.

Of course she can't move, she's clipped her own financial wings. She's trapped. She's learned the difference between choosing to slum somewhere and having to, and it's made her think of the child she will have. (One child maximum, after she's thirty and definitely before she's forty.)

Naturally this would be unthinkable in Hackney, but hardly more tolerable in one of the more affluent areas of London where there are – "nauseating middle-class ghettos full of dimmer switches, panic buttons and kids behind burglar bars."

As for the English countryside, "nothing left of it, just one big suburbia overrun with cars and garden centres."

She begins to dream of a place unclogged by traffic, a landscape of tranquil communities where children can run barefoot and free range.
A place where Culture and Style go hand in hand, where the business of Living is taken seriously, where food isn't full of chemicals. Where property is dirt cheap.

COUNTRY HOMES
AND INTERIORS
French Special
Dordogne
WORLD OF
ERIORS
Calvados
du Pays d'
Foie de Veau
1Kg 00,50 F
SAUCISSE
DE MONTAGNE

Normandy

D*ans la vie*, one way or another, we often get what we ask for, sometimes unexpectedly. Gemma needed money.
It was at this point her father dropped dead from a heart attack leaving his daughter feeling "alone . . . totally gutted."
But also richer by some £65,000, plus an extra £5,000 – the sum put aside for the "proper" wedding she had rejected.
Gemma went to Reading and wept with her stepmother.

For months she wrote nothing in her journal, so who knows the extent of her grief?
By the next entry, it's evident she'd been in France looking at property.
It finds her weighing up two houses – one in the Pas de Calais, the other in Normandy. She chose Normandy. Bought it outright, didn't bother with a mortgage. She contributed £55,000, Charlie the rest.

COUNTRY
DECO

All along it seems Charlie had misgivings. As soon as the deal was done, these doubts turned into panic, the blackest pessimism. Every night Gemma reassured him, every night she re-painted the picture: a life of rustic bliss over the Channel . . . the wine, the food, the veg they would grow, the work they would do, the friends who would stay, the baby they might have. . . .

BAILLEVILLE – 31 km ROUEN
Maison normande comprenant cuisine, séjour avec cheminée, autre pièce. A l'étage 3 chambres, salle de bain, WC. Chauffage électrique. Dépendance usage d'atelier. Terrain 1 ha 38.
Prix: 670 000

Charlie's Panic:

- Losing the London apartment

You won't, Charlie....we sublet to Colin...the agents won't know. IF they ask questions, he's my cousin and we're away on holiday...

- Having to pay French tax

You can avoid it...It's easy - if you don't register, they don't know about you... We just go on being taxed in England...

- Not speaking French

Doesn't matter...not for work... Work will still come from London..yours'll still come via your brother ...Just be a longer drive for you, when you deliver stuff....

- The van won't cope

We'll get another van - a newer one for the hard driving. Keep the old one for fun.... we can afford it...

- Telling his ex-wife

Having the kids on her own!...she'll KILL me! ..she'll disembowel me!!
Charlie, she routinely disembowels you when you spend 24 hours a day doing everything she asks!
You'll never please her. - She needs you to be in the wrong...so why not genuinely be in the wrong for once?

- Missing his children

You'll see them every ten days...they'll come in the holidays..and at half term..and...
But you don't understand...

It's OK for you, but I can't just up sticks! I can't leave them..I can't do it...

Think of the barn, Charlie–it'll make you a terrific workshop....

..think how cheap WINE is there..and ciggies! France is brilliant for smokers... .... think of..

Charlie's Workshop
London E2

...Judi, Gemma and I thought it'd be terribly good for Justin and Delia's **French**, if we sublet Hotwell Street and bought a place in France... ...just the other end of the Tunnel, so they could just pop over...
Judi... ~~we~~... Gemma's just sort of got a very small house in France...

Lyre Grove
London N1

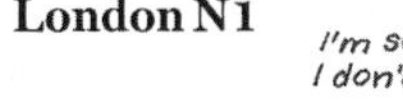

I'm so angry, Charlie I don't know what to...

...You can't afford to increase the kids' maintenance...but you **can** afford a new van and a French holiday home...

What the hell am I meant to think?!!!
Van's second hand..it's not a holiday home.... going to **work** there.. ..and it's Gemma who

Yes, it's her money... ...but you said **You** contributed a bit....

SAVINGS, Charlie??? How've you managed that? Just how much've you been salting away??

Bugger all, after what I give you

So you think that entitles you to go to France...leave me to bring up the kids single-handed?!!!
But I'll be over a **lot**, Judi!

*I mean! what sort of father **ARE YOU**?!!*

We may do..may not. If we do, France is better for kids than East London...
*How you have the **GALL** to think of having a second family*

Oh I can see that...

You certainly wouldn't want to have a child **cooped up**, breathing London smog and going to a **sink school**, would you?
Not a lot, no.

Funny...you never worry about **OUR** kids doing that..do you?!!
HYPOCRITE!
*Judee! They do **NOT** go to **sink** sch...*

***How** can you do this to them?!! How can you abandon your children like this?!..move thousands of miles away! ..... just waltz out of their lives! How can you do this to **ME**?*
O.K. Go to France, then.. ***Rat*** on your kids ***Rat*** on your responsibilities...
But I think you'll **REGRET** it!
Sorry?
You HEARD!

So, of all the timbered houses in Normandy, the Boverys bought the one just down the lane from us.

All we knew at first was that they were foreign, and that was hardly interesting. English, Dutch, Germans, Belgians – there are more and more round here. Second-home owners. They come and go. The better kind stimulate the local economy, including my shop, so one shouldn't complain. The worst kind – and they're often English – arrive with their cars stuffed from the hypermarket. They spend a week or two at a time, like little milords in splendid isolation. And they never bother to learn French. No wonder I wasn't excited.

Until Gemma and Charlie moved in.

Martine! Martine!
Dévines quoi! Guess what!

Madame Bovary's next door!!!
I mean it! They're English, but they're called BOVARY!

BOVARY!..incroyable, non?

No reaction at all. But then neither my wife nor my son have any feeling whatsoever for literature. Pascal complains that the book's too long and the heroine is a disgusting mother. Martine's only comment is that Madame Bovary herself is a pain.

I don't know why, but talk of books really irritates Martine. For instance, in company, whenever I discuss a text, or the world of publishing, she's always very quick to point out that I had been merely an editor of school text books. For use in Africa.

I would not like to suggest that Martine and I didn't get on. We'd been seven years in Bailleville, and though the provincial round was a little slow, I could say quite truthfully that neither of us missed our old life in Paris.

I moved on to other important details of our new British neighbours.

* Mais comme elle est belle! ...Elle doit avoir presque quarante ans!
Madame Bovary?

* SHE'S SO BEAUTIFUL!..AND SHE MUST BE NEARLY 40!

Non, non!..not HER!– she's about thirty...rather fat... ..No..her VAN! Old VW van ...beautiful! Lovely condition!

The husband also has a van...a recent model..not interesting...
Hnh! You've really been snooping, haven't you?

Snooping? What d'you mean!?

O don't give me that! You were spying on them...

I hate the way you spy on people!
I do not SPY!

L'aube s'annonce au Serengeti....
O, come on! You admit it yourself! You said the best thing about working at Pelletier was spotting office romances....

...après une gestation de 20 à 22 mois, la femelle...
You and your Nature documentaries!.... ..spend your whole life hoping to see something mating...

It wasn't until they came into my shop in Bailleville that I saw Gemma and Charles Bovery at close quarters.

It pleased me that Madame stood for some moments in rapture, in reverence, transported by . . . *une volupté pure*, as she breathed the rich, warm aromas of my bread.

Boulangerie Joubert

Bloody hell, Charlie!...I mean, **25 different** kinds of bread! God, the French are incredible! I mean, they just know how to **live**!
Mmm..!
God, this is serious bread!
mmnnh! It **tastes**! ...tastes **REAL**!

She was right. I make <u>real</u> bread, full of taste and texture, not white factory stuff. And if I do nothing else in my life but perpetuate the love of good honest bread, then I shall be content. Bread for me is a passion. It is our patrimony. To hold bread in one's hands, to feel its surface – each crest, ridge, valley, fissure, crevasse, is to feel the earth, the primeval crust where life began. It is to bathe one's senses in the colour and smell of ripened corn. It is to taste sunlight. Nothing is more natural, more humble than bread. Nothing is more <u>sensual</u>.

C'est la nature! ...la santé... ...la vie!
Boulangerie JOUBERT
PAIN A L'ANCIENNE
25 sortes de pain frais au jour

But I digress. It seemed that Gemma found everything about her new life in Normandy entrancing. One saw her in the market exclaiming over the vegetables, one heard her singing in the garden.
It was early summer.
Nestling in its green embrace, their little house, with smoke curling from the chimney, resembled the last scene of a fairy tale, the page where the protagonists will live happily ever after.

I remember that both Martine and I had the same thought:

They won't last long...two bad winters, they'll be off...
Ah. Oui

We'd seen it all before, this bourgeois fantasy. Foreigners – they move to France, bury themselves in their hectare of mud and wonder why they go mad.

Actually, as my wife pointed out, I was in no position to sneer at the Boverys. After all, I'd been a city refugee myself, not once, but twice.

The first time was thirty years ago. I left Paris, where I'd been a student, and drove south in my 2CV*....

* called "**PANTA RHEI**" from the phrase of Heraclitus **EVERYTHING FLOWS**

... and in the Lozère I lived *en commune* with friends and goats, making cheese, smoking joints, and thinking. (The book I never wrote grew and grew in my head.)

Who am I to presume to answer the question: **Who am I ??**

Eight months later I was back in Paris... a matter of conscience. Bit by bit it had become *un vrai camp de faschos*, with their mania for rules. Plus, it was cold, and I'd got boils.

It was then that the poetry drained from my life. The next eighteen years I worked for Editions Pelletier off the Boulevard St Germain. I met Martine Morin, a market researcher, in Crete. We married. We had two sons, Jean and Pascal. We lived in a small apartment in the quartier Tolbiac...

... until seven years ago, when Pelletier was taken over, and I was kicked out. For the second time I left Paris, and with Martine and the boys came back here to my roots in Normandy – to Bailleville, where after a while, and to everyone's surprise, I reversed the fortunes of the family *boulangerie*, which had flagged since my father's death.

Perhaps it's in the blood, but quite simply I'd fallen in love with bread, the sort of bread I'd seen in certain shops in Paris. AUTHENTIC bread, bio-bread, bread that's five hours in the making. *Le bon pain*. The sort of bread that breathes integrity, history, nostalgia – the sort of bread that made Gemma Bovery, the first time I saw her, sink her teeth into it right there in the shop...

Pain de Dieppe

God...bloody amazing shop, this...
Bloody expensive if you ask me

Oh, come on, Charlie! It's worth it...you never get bread like this in England...it's **REAL**... ..it's....

Something I found a little sexy at the time – she seemed so hungry and alive.

Mmm! Mnyumm!! MnnMMM...

But now when I recall that image (as I often do) it makes me shudder. It keeps me awake. It burns holes in my sleep. It reminds me of all the bad shit that was to come.

Three Seasons

Bailleville, Normandy

June 19. Bought loads of broad beans in the market. The woman said was I making "une bonne soupe aux fèves". (I was!) God, I love shopping here - its so HUMAN! People pass the time of day. You feel part of things. I don't know ANYWHERE in England where you can walk down the road and find 5 kinds of potato - and everything's FRESH & not covered in bloody shrink wrap. The French are so civilised! It's heaven here - no papers, no T.V. - Actually we tried putting on our telly for the first time this evening and it doesn't WORK over here - French signal is different or something, Charlie says. Tant pis!

E.LECLERC

October 29. Kid's Half Term.
Told Charlie this is the last time they come here. Next holidays they can bloody stay in London and moan at their mother. I KNOW it's boring here - the country IS boring. I'M bored - bored stiff with the same shops and faces & spending my life cooking stuff they go YUK! at. Drove to Rouen today & did week's shop in Le Clerc - so much quicker & cheaper. They can stuff themselves sick on oven chips from now on.

January 5th.
Began DIET. Weigh nearly 70 kilos. Hate myself. Freezing day inside & out. Van wouldn't start so had to shop locally. Went to the furthest chemist cos I can't bear the one near the Mairie - nosy bitch always looks at me when I buy Tampax, like she's thinking "Not pregnant yet, then?" There's no privacy in this bloody one-eyed place!

The reasons for Gemma Bovery's disenchantment fall into five categories:

1. The House

Of course, it needed serious reconstruction. But the Boverys, beyond some plumbing and rewiring, did nothing. Perhaps it was lack of money – more likely it was Gemma's mania for preserving the Authentic, the patina of Time.

She must, however, have spent a pile on the contents – all kinds of *cochonneries*, some brought from England, some found in France: ancient quilts, linens, milking stools, lambing chairs, flails, gelding irons.

As the diary indicates, it was the assemblage of these objects that gave Gemma her happiest hours. No Old Dutch Master could have put more effort into the arrangements of *nature morte*. To Gemma it was the creation of a sort of perfection, a simple goodness which she could imagine rubbing off on Life itself.

But when it was done the result looked . . .

like a sodding antique shop...
TWEE.. **corny**... **PHONY**...
total total crap...

Other problems announced themselves: mice, moths, mites, woodworm, wet rot, damp, cracks, leaks. It was too small, too dark. There was a brownish light, like living in a pencil box. There was no privacy. You heard people in the WC and when guests stayed the drains blocked. No one came to stay more than once, except Charlie's kids, who were of course obliged to come each holiday. But while they articulated their disgust, Gemma kept hers to herself, as much as she could. She couldn't complain. The whole thing had been her idea. Her choice.

I keep expecting Charlie to start blaming me for making us buy this tip – but he doesn't – he avoids saying anything, which is far worse. He never complains. He's just completely detached, like the house isn't his problem. If I point out some disaster, he plays it down... humours me. Really patronising.. really pisses me off.

Leak or two.. it's what you tend to find...

..old house..empty for a few months... you expect the odd problem...

Not like this I didn't!

Charlie! It's **COLD**... **DAMP**... it stinks of sewage...and it's riddled with **VERMIN**!

...I mean, things couldn't 've been **much** worse for the original peasants here...back whenever it was...

O probably they **were**... you know..failed harvests... famine...Black Death...
Oh, great
..that's something to look forward to, then..

Reasons for Gemma Bovery's disenchantment:

2. Mark and Wizzy Rankin

DARLING! MARK! MAR-ARK!
TWO gigots ..OK ?
What?
GET WHAT?
TWO?
OK darling

One always knew when the Rankins were over from England. One saw the Range Rover, the number plate MR 2, and one always made the same *plaisanterie.*

MR 2...
emmerdeur

...so, how many are we for lunch..? 14... or perhaps 16...Sam and Polly may drop in on their way home from Périgueux...

..deux tartes avec prunes..um... and trwah tartes aux pommes ...er...um..and..er weet baguettes

Gemma tried to avoid them – she hadn't come to Normandy 'to meet Brits and whining Brit-brats'.

But inevitably, in a small place like Bailleville they did meet. This meeting led to drinks, which in turn led to both Charlie and Gemma finding welcome employment at the Rankins' *manoir* – LES PORTAILS – Charlie distressing their over-restored antiques, and Gemma painting *faux marbre* in the bathrooms.

There was plenty about the Rankins for Gemma to find repugnant:

Mark's enormous annual bonus; the colour scheme: the telephone boxes by the pool (shower and changing cabin); their fleet of mahogany *lits bateaux*; their other houses in London and Verbier; the nanny and domestics who allow Wizzy (latterly a head-hunter) to play perfect mother and hostess. The house parties; guests who never cry off their visits, like Gemma's, but who swarm across the Channel – sisters, aunts, nephews, cousins, Mark's fellow corporate financiers; bond traders in drovers' coats; journalists, men going through mucky divorces (Wizzy's speciality). The table laid for 25 . . . The excess, the waste, the empties . . . The smell of serious money, the whiff of the metropolis.

.. but with this one, thought I'd have a break... stay at home. Yes, I DO miss work... but you can't have everything can you?

It made Gemma feel sick. But not only that, it tainted her view of her own circumstances, made her dream cottage seem even smaller, darker and more squalid. And made her and Charlie's Simple Life seem a form of self-punishment – joyless, friendless, reclusive, boring.

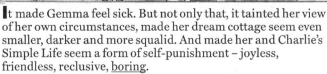

Reasons for Gemma Bovery's disenchantment:

3. Fear

Her diary makes it quite plain: after the first rapturous weeks, the house and the surrounding *paysage* filled Gemma with nervosity.

..just can't stand it at night – when Charlie's away I sleep with the light on – which is pathetic, but can't help it. I KNOW what the noises are – the dog, mice, woodworm, roof leaking etc. but they still get me... that horrible creaking – sounds like someone's inching their way upstairs in a leather coat.

Outside was equally disturbing: Gemma claims that when she went out sketching the landscape somehow immobilised her. After a while she couldn't draw. Anything. This doesn't surprise me. Normandy was, after all, the great outdoor *atelier* of the nineteenth century. How could one not be reminded of those giants of painting– Millet, Monet, etc? How could one not feel inhibited, one's efforts absolutely pigmy?

So on the day when she described herself sitting hunched at the edge of a harvest field, it was perhaps the thought of Monet's *Haystacks* that froze her drawing hand.

No reason at all I get totally freaked. Today it started with seeing a tick in the bracken – remembered reading tick bites are bad news.. also bracken spores give you cancer. Then couldn't stop hearing every rustle & twig snap behind me.. Started thinking: Rabid animals... rapists... ...French murders, like in the papers – Killer is always local half-wit garagiste or else bloke in coat who asks the time....

Fox?
That's the trouble with the country ..just makes you PARANOID – like everywhere looks like those places you see on CRIMEWATCH – idyllic leafy places where the body's found, where the police put up a sinister little tent.

Reasons for Gemma Bovery's disenchantment:

4. Pharmacies, etc.

Pharmacie

It's weird- the French have chemists like England has sweetshops – they're bloody everywhere, even in a one-eyed place like Bailleville.

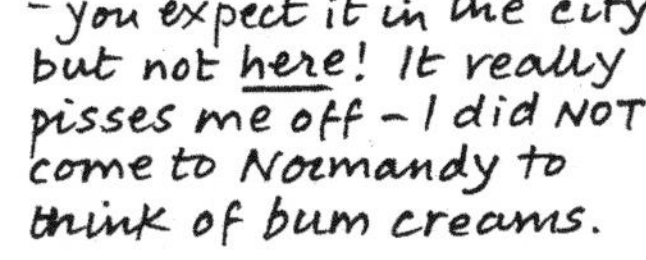

And everywhere you get bombarded with body propaganda – you expect it in the city but not here! It really pisses me off – I did NOT come to Normandy to think of bum creams.

....pour après la douche... c'est une crème lifting bio-suractivée...c'est à dire...

RMACIE

PHARMACIE

OENOBIOL
HYDRA+

Percutaféine gel
Contre la cellulite
Pour agir au bon endroit

Salon de Beauté
VISAGISTE
Eclat de beauté
BIOSTHETIQUE

What's great about England- if you want to, you can go for days looking complete crap – and no one notices. Here, you get looked at like you're seriously deviant — by locals too, not just weekenders, – Princess Caroline clones with Paris number plates. French really do believe in poncing up 24 hours a day. Exfoliating really is a national pastime... The strain of it! The time it must take them. Nauseating.

Weird how Fr. women, almost without exception, have new handbags.

Cosm

Promincil

Note: The *pharmacie* that Gemma used most frequently during this period is the one where my cousin works. Cousine Jeanne, who remembers everything about everybody. Later on, it was from her that I learned that Madame Bovery took the Pill (and of her husband's athlete's foot).

Reasons for Gemma Bovery's disenchantment:

5. Charlie.

He began to infuriate her.
He was so enthusiastic about everything. So pleased with Bailleville, so relentlessly optimistic about the house and all its defects (cracks, leaks, the smell of ordure).
And while every day Gemma felt increasingly restless and bored, every day Charlie, it seemed to her, looked more and more the picture of French rustic bliss (the very bliss she had dangled before him all those months ago in London) and the more he did so the more *emmerdant* she found him.

..It's just a few hiccups, Gemma... ...we'll sort them out...
BAR TABAC LE
LOTO
TABAC
ENGLISH SPOKEN
CHARLIE BOVERY
MEUBLES et BOISERIE
RESTAURATION
VERNISSAGE

His beret, she writes, made him look "a complete berk, like someone in a Stella Artois ad." He smelt of Gauloises, ate in his vest, put Calvados in his coffee. His smile was stuck at sleepy. She thought he was turning into a vegetable, a turnip. She found less and less to say to him.

And perhaps he didn't have much to say to her, because he wasn't often in the house. Often he was away altogether – in London, seeing his kids; delivering restored and picking up unrestored things at his brother's antique shop. Mostly he was in the barn, for hours on end.

I, Joubert, often remarked the light still on at midnight. I supposed some Stakhanovite regime of work. Gemma did not. He would be "playing Doom, Minesweeper and Solitaire on his computer . . . playing tunes on his teeth . . . and doing crosswords in the papers the Rankins save for him. Happy as a pig in shit."

I rather doubt he was. I remember on one occasion asking after his wife, and seeing his expression change from sleepy to hunted, his eyes like something peering out of a dark hole.

TICK-TACK TICKETTY TACK
SIGH
ANAGRAM GNATS =
ANGST
...if she doesn't want a baby.... what does she want..?
Patrick Hi.. it's ME
Gemma? God, how are you? long time no....

As yet, in all these pages of Gemma's diary, I've only discovered one reference to myself. Strange, because for a time she saw me daily – not so often in the *boulangerie*. Her enthusiasm for the unhurried intimacies of local shopping didn't last. Very soon we noticed her weekly trip to the supermarket in Rouen.

It was in the afternoons that we met, while walking our respective dogs. Gemma always did the same circuit and soon, I admit, it wasn't by coincidence that our paths crossed. I planned the encounters, but always with discretion. The truth is, Mrs Bovery fascinated me. It had nothing to do with her appearance. Her clothes were *atroce*, and in those days she was fat, like a big English bun. What I found compelling about her was her **NAME**.

It amused me to greet her, with a slight bow, "*Bonjour*, Madame **BOVARY**!" She always looked at me blankly, as if the reference meant nothing to her. But reading her diary I now realise that this wasn't the case. She was thinking of reverting to her maiden name because "everyone from the bloody baker upwards comments on Madame Bovary, it's so boring."

Well, what did she expect, living here? We're not peasants. We know our literature. We read books, some of us even try to write them. I, myself, the baker she refers to so slightingly, have in the past written on Freemasonry and Revolution in 18th-century Rouen. When I left university there was talk of publishing my dissertation.

After my fourth or fifth encounter I tested her . . .

You know, your name-it 'as great resonance in France.. literary resonance!...
.le chef d'oeuvre de **Flaubert**!
....
Oui. Je sais. c'est un film...
...er.. non... c'est un livre

Mais..vous ne l'avez pas **lu** ?!

er...non...mon français n'est pas bon...

(The arrogance. They come here to live but make not the least effort to engage with the culture.)

A few weeks later Gemma changed her daily routine. Perhaps she walked elsewhere, I don't know, but for months I saw her only at a distance, walking morosely to the Poste in a big coat or pacing up and down their garden. Then, one day in August, as I was sheltering from a rainstorm in the woods above Bailleville and I heard these anguished sighs. I saw the dog Carrington and then HER. I thought, My God, she's got THIN. In my experience, one thing above all makes a woman sigh and waste away. It was then I permitted myself the idle fancy that Gemma Bovery, like her literary namesake, was in love.

Je suis prêt à parier ma couille gauche qu'elle a un amant..*
* I'll bet she's got a lover

The diary tells me it wasn't Love that made Gemma lose weight, but merely diet and exercise (of a most horrible rigour).
What prompted her to do it? Boredom and self-disgust, certainly; narcissism or self-punishment, perhaps.
It seems to have been a preparation not only for flight but also for staying put.
She writes of leaving France, of working in London – or in New York. But then she writes of staying here, of integrating, of learning the language, of living in Paris. Or Provence.
She writes of leaving her husband, but then of staying with him, of "giving it another go."
She is in a turmoil of indecision, going backwards and forwards, backwards and forwards.

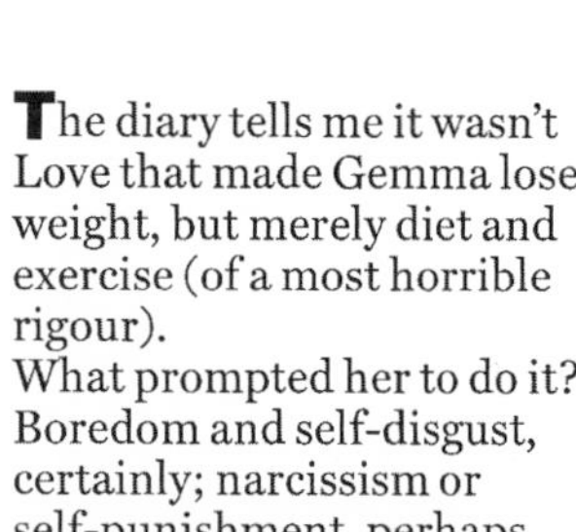

...j'aurais voulu...
..tu aurais voulu...
...il aurait voulu...
...nous aurions voulu....

Wizzy'll be here soon ...where's your better half, Charlie?
Upstairs.... learning French
Oh. Going **native**, is she?......
Mmm..ah, this is the Life! **BLOODY** nice!
Just like HOME..'cept better...
Well, **I** like it.... Wizzy's not so sure, now...she'd prefer Something in the **Loire** - somewhere warmer
I just think it's too bloody far for weekends, ...the Loire...
Pwuuh! God, Charlie, **that** your fosse septique?
Well, it's **not** my after-shave
'**Struth!** Smells like a **cut price** sewage farm!
Quelle belle smell!

Tuesday p.m.
20 mins inner thighs.
Also practised verbs, venir & vouloir. Learnt conditional.
In a minute I suppose I'll have to go down and be nice to the bloody Rankins.
Can't face it... but whatever happens, I need to earn some money. Wizzy said she wanted me to do the stencils in her kitchen. Probably her usual crap taste so will have to grit my teeth. Thing is, the Rankins are LOADED but they're bloody mean. They treat Charlie like a sort of caretaker — always ringing up from London, asking him to send on mail, get leaves out of gutters etc. But they don't pay him and he doesn't seem to mind. God, I can hear him and Mark now. Sometimes I think I'm in Surrey not France.

...Oh, he's missed it! ..tried to work the ball away to Square Leg, but mis timed it... And England still wobbling at 211 for 5...
...coming in now...given it bags of air...it's squirted out on the on-side..it's in the **AIR**!....**He's CAUGHT**! Out caught by....
Oh..**what** a **plonker**! ..**what** an ocean-going plonker!

Later. God *awful* evening. Rankins were here, boozing with Charlie outside. Stink from the drains was really FOUL — You couldn't breathe downstairs. Whole house smelt like a PORTA-LOO. Wizzy had brought one of her crappy "Bundles from Britain" – Marmite, Weetabix, last week's Sunday Times. I was hiding in the sitting room, having a read and she came in and started droning on about the bloody house....

...You know you really ought to take it up professionally, Gemma...you're say clever! ...adore the way you've done it..it's say lovely and....peasanty...
You must **LOVE** living here!

Gemma? You must **love** it here...
No, I don't. I hate it...

WHY-Y? Godsake! s'only a blocked drain! **Super** here!

D'you miss **LONDON**? That it? Golly, ***KNOW*** **I** would, if **WE** were over here full time...must get **LONELY**!
See, I think you need loads of people staying, for it to be fun!

Don't **want** people staying - I want to know people **here**!

FRENCH?? Oh God, they're ***frightfully*** difficult to know...
...unless you know them already
I mean, they're jolly friendly in shops ..and our builders are **sweet**!....
...but other **Frogs**, they aren't bothered...
...well, ***why should*** they?

I was reading the STYLE bit. Wizzy goes "Friend of ours is in that, used to live next door in Elgin Crescent, lives in Clerkenwell now.. Pandora.." I nearly fainted.. God, there's this whole bloody article about them – Pandora and **Patrick!!** He's married her!! Bastard! He's married with a baby! I just couldn't handle it, thought I was going to throw up....

THE SUNDAY TIMES
STYLE
Frock Horror

God, Mark, D'know **WHAT** I said, but she just rushed out of the room. ***Honestly! Bloody RUDE!***
Not surprised, living in that depressing dump...s'like an agricultural museum
She's so neurotic!
God, yes **GHASTLY!**

Poor Gemma, tossing all night, the magazine article (the very one I found in her diary) looming in her sleep like some monstrous billboard.

There he was, her ex-lover, his newish wife and baby, the Corbusier chair, and the white radiance of their vast apartment.
And there was Gemma, waking to the grey tedium of her marriage and to the feculence of her bad drains.

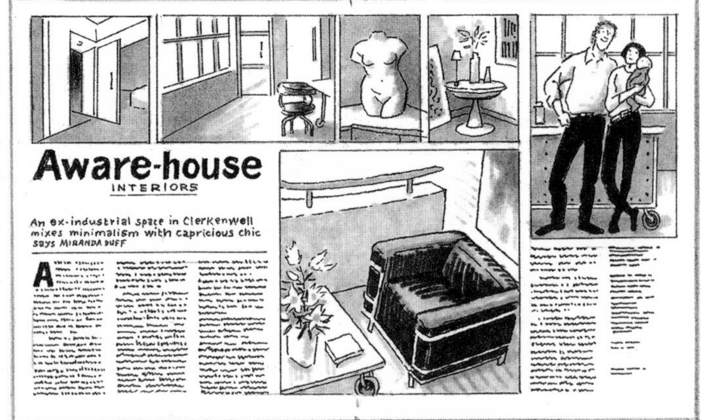

Aware-house

INTERIORS

An ex-industrial space in Clerkenwell mixes minimalism with capricious chic says MIRANDA DUFF

Wednesday. Early

Wish I didn't know..wish I'd never seen it. Could've gone on dreaming. But now he's married!! Patrick married. He's such a hypocrite!!! Said he didn't believe in marriage, said he never wanted kids. It's just so SICK Suppose it's HER money, her connections.. he's such a snob. Looks so smug, pleased with himself. Self-basting sod. Thinks he's got it all. Well it won't last, knowing him. But I can't bear it, it's ~~torture~~ TORTURE!! I wanted HIM, I wanted that. I loved him!!! Why couldn't he have loved me?

Mnnh..what day is it, Gemma?
Wednesday, Charlie...

Thought I'd sort the drains out...go into Bailleville..get a plunger...hire some drain rods..or maybe, ask about a plumber.....
Oh, I would've done that, darling
I'm sure you would, Charlie... in your own good time....

Boulangerie Joubert
PAIN DE SON
PAIN RUSTIQUE
PAIN DE DIEPPE
PAIN BUCHERON
PAIN AU PAVOT
PAIN AUX NOIX
PAIN AU SESAME
BOULE AU LEVAIN
PAIN A L'ANCIENNE
25 SORTES DE PAIN FRAIS AUJOUR
LOTO
...What is a PLUNGER? plongeur?...quelquechose pour un lavabo bloqué? .. un bloquage dans le W.C? ... DRAINS... what ARE drains..?... égouts...

I remember the day very well. It was the first time I saw Gemma Bovery's legs.

Gemma! Cuckoo!
Hiyee! GEMMAH!!

Gemma! Do look! I've found something really brill for your drains pong!

I knew the stall. It sells soaps, candles, body scrubs. Overpriced *cochonneries* smelling of tarmac and low tide. And I knew the things Madame Parkin sniffed with such rapture – room sprays of a grotesque pungency: "Fireside" or "Washed Linen" or "*Pain d'Épices*" – The "Scents of Childhood." *C'est du sous-Proust pour les cons de bourgeois.*

Here! Smell this one!.... "Cuisine de Mamie".... S'AMAYZING!! Smells just like BREAD BAKING!!
Les Arômes de l'Enfance

There's a sort of smoky one... "Coin du Feu"... and this one... "Baisers de Maman"... doesn't that mean Mummy's kisses? ...Oh POO! God... smells like lipstick!
Mum!
Mummee!
Mummee-e!

STOP SHOUTING Allegra! What IS it?!
Owh! Daddy says HURRY UP! He wants to GO!

Sorry Gemma! Must dash! Got to take the eeny-wees home.... Come on Humpty! Off we go, darling!

Gemma just stood there. She looked so bored, so fed up. A few days before, I'd been convinced she was love sick. Thinking it over, I wasn't so sure. One would have known if she had a lover here in Bailleville. One would have seen the comings and goings.
Now it struck me that her trouble might be <u>lack</u> of love – not enough sex.
What she needed was . . .
It was then that I noticed Hervé de Bressigny also standing there like a dummy.
Something very strange happened. The second after my eyes rested upon him it was as if, like a film director, I had shouted "ACTION!" He came to life. He spoke to Gemma!
It was as if I had <u>willed</u> him to do it, and as if I had directed Gemma to . . .

Pwuhh!

Ca sent mauvais?
Sorry?

It smells bad?
Yeah! It does! This one's better... smells of hot bread

Their conversation lasted about two minutes, during which I heard Gemma laugh for the first time. And Hervé – well, I had seen him for a fair bit of his idle young life, but never before so animated, so <u>interested</u>.

Boulangerie Joubert

I watched Gemma until she disappeared up rue Crochet, then turned my attention to Hervé de Bressigny.

PAIN AU BUCHERON
PAIN AU PAVOT
PAIN AUX NOIX
PAIN AU SESAME
BOULEAU LEVANT

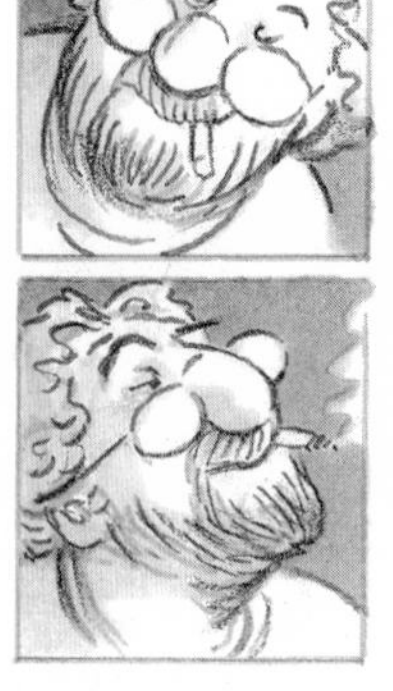

Joubert

He (1) put his dark glasses on; (2) grinned slightly; (3) combed his hair with his fingers; (4) tossed his forelock back (unfortunately dislodging the glasses); (5) lit a contemplative cigarette, which burned him when it stuck to his lip. I identified these signs, this unconscious rhetoric: Hervé was steamed up by his encounter with Gemma.

!

With hindsight how I wish they'd never met. How I wish Hervé had cleared off to Paris, which is where he spends most of the time with his widowed mother and two sisters.

These days the Bressignys hardly use La Boissière, the decaying barracks of a chateau one sees just off the main road here, its park full of ragwort and dead timber. But when they are in residence, my niece Crystelle helps in the kitchen. And consequently hears a thing or two.

This is how I knew that Hervé was revising for a law exam, one he'd failed in the summer and was due to retake in September. According to Crystelle, his mother had yelled at him that he wasn't coming back with them to Paris. He was to stay on in Normandy for a week or so and complete his revision. She wasn't having him nightclubbing. He was to stay put and work his arse off. He had to pass this time, or else.

Knowing this, I remember feeling a strange glee. It meant that Hervé and Gemma might meet again. I confess my imagination had raced ahead: I already saw them in naked embrace. Something which made me laugh out loud. The absurdity of it. Life imitating Flaubert's masterpiece: Madame Bovary crosses the path of the local squire, Rodolphe, just as Gemma, a few minutes ago, had crossed Hervé's.

PAIN A L'ANCIENNE
25 SORTES DE PAIN
FRAIS AU JOUR
!

Well, I say "just as," but it was of course nothing like the novel – Life rarely imitates Art. Art has some point to it, whereas Life . . .

I was deep in my scrutiny of Hervé, when my wife came up to the shop door and jabbed me in the ribs.

Ogling **men**, now?... ...aren't **girls** enough any more?...

Do some **WORK!** Vraiment, tu deviens de plus en plus **con!**

According to the diary, Gemma returned from the market that day intending "to really talk to Charlie." Certainly about the idea of selling up and returning to England and maybe the idea of a trial separation. She couldn't stand their not talking any more.
But when she got home she found Charlie had done two surprising things: first, he'd telephoned someone to come and unblock the septic tank. Second, he'd organised a small *soirée*, a dinner party whose imminence made Gemma forget her serious talk, *un petit diner* to which Charlie had invited me, Joubert, and my wife.

...oh, and I'd better check - either of you vegan..vegetarian...?
Comment?

Martine and I spent some time debating the motive for this sudden invitation. Martine thought the Boverys had come to realise their isolation.

Mais ils vont parler en anglais tout le temps...really, I'm not up to a whole evening of that... Anyway, we don't know them!
But I said we'd go, Martine!... Listen, we'll insist they speak French ....

I don't know why I began to look forward to the evening. But I did. After all, a meal – the offering of food under another's roof – signals the beginning of intimacy.
I remember looking across to the Boverys, imagining Charlie telling Gemma we were coming, imagining her perhaps already planning the menu. And the thought of her, *une anglaise*, having to ponder what I, Joubert, might like to eat, I found strangely erotic.

But I thought you'd be PLEASED!..You moan you're bored..you moan you never meet any French!...I mean, God! What DO you want, Gemma!?
But the Jouberts and the Sanniers... we don't know them, Charlie!
KIDNEY
MUNG

We buy Joubert's bread and Sannier was our notaire...but that's all...and they may hate each other!...Can't imagine what we'll talk about!.... Anyway, I'm not so keen on Joubert – he's always staring at me, dirty old sod...
And now I've got to give him dinner! Great!

Listen, I'll do it all... all the cooking, Gemma Yeah? I'll do something very, very simple...

No, not simple, Charlie..all we ever eat is simple... I've done fart food... done PEASANT...
.....how about Bloody Extravagant for a change...?

Could do my curry...
No Charlie...you can't invite French and then dynamite their insides...
marie claire
THE RIVER
THE RIVER CAFE COOKBOOK

Most Saturdays I'm in Rouen. We sell bread in the market. The day of the Boverys' dinner was no exception. In the late afternoon I remember driving home to Bailleville in a dirty light, the sky behind me dark with thunderclouds.
As I neared the town, I came up behind a familiar vehicle.

TOOT TTTOOT!

Allo G.B.!....
...âllo Gemma Bovery!

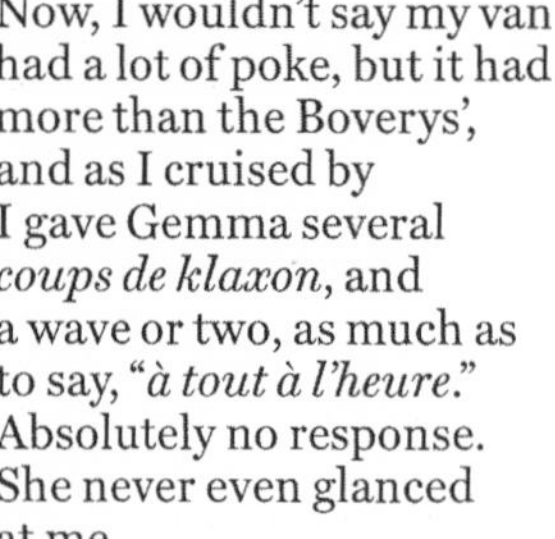
Now, I wouldn't say my van had a lot of poke, but it had more than the Boverys', and as I cruised by I gave Gemma several *coups de klaxon*, and a wave or two, as much as to say, "*à tout à l'heure*." Absolutely no response. She never even glanced at me.

But I watched her. I watched the image that vibrated in my mirror – a tiny cinema screen where Gemma in her asthmatic van seemed to crawl before the storm . And all the while an infinity of blackness gained and gathered, hanging overhead like some awful fate.

Did I read in that image a portent of tragedy?
Well . . . I thought any minute now it's going to piss like cows on a flat rock. Then, seeing the woods of La Boissière and the chateau itself, I thought of Hervé de Bressigny – not as he was in real life (callow, conventional, closeted somewhere in that dank pile revising matrimonial law). No. In my mind he'd become a suave seducer, flexing his fingers in anticipation.

I shall never know what came over me, or quite why, but passing the entrance to the chateau, I was aware of speaking aloud, aware of addressing the VW van behind me: "*Allez, tournez à gauche*," I commanded.

S'cré nom de PETIT BONHOMME!

At that moment the horizon detonated in a great boom of thunder, so loud I ducked. When I looked in the mirror, *voilà*! The obedient van had turned and was disappearing through the gateway of La Boissière.

Imagine my feelings. Shock. Glee. Utter mystification. Was it my doing or what? And if it wasn't, what was Gemma up to visiting that *petit con*? She didn't know him and, more to the point, what about her *soirée*? She'd invited us for 8 o'clock.

Il est déjà six heures trente...elle devrait préparer le dîner!!

Mais qu'est-ce qu'elle fout là?.... C'est monstrueux!!!

By 8pm I was mad with curiosity to see Gemma. But when we arrived at the Boverys Charlie announced that she was running a bit late – she'd only just got back from Rouen, where the storm had held her up. Ah, I thought, already she's telling lies. She hasn't told him about stopping off at the chateau for an hour and a quarter with young Bressigny.

(I timed her, you see. 78 minutes from when I saw her turn off to La Boissière and when she drove home past my house. 78 minutes doing what, exactly? Perhaps something entirely innocent. But what? – What does a married woman do alone with a young man in a thunderstorm?)

Gemma kept to the kitchen, where we heard a clattering of pans. Meanwhile we, her guests, endured an endless aperitif.

(Besides Martine and myself, there were four others, all local. The English Rankins I couldn't object to – they are, after all, excellent customers of mine. But the Sanniers – *merde*! Smug right-wing bores. He was the notaire when the Boverys bought their house.)

Ça est Pimms, tu say... c'est tray, tray anglay avec GIN dedans!
Ah bon
C'est quoi "Monsieur Porky?"
PIMM'S No1 CUP
MR. PORKY
PORK SCRATCHINGS
KrNZ! Krntz!
et..la Reine Mère – elle a quelle âge maintenant?
Um....

Of that tedious hour I remember the following details:

- The drink – sickly. Bladder-filling.
- "Scratchings", brought by Mrs Rankin from England. Noisy. Tasting of pig. Salty. Thirst-making.
- The talk – absolutely cretinous.
- M. Sannier's nauseatingly fluent English. (As I suppose it should be, since he spends his time helping foreigners buy up bits of France.)
- Mme Sannier immaculate in pink linen. The English in their dirty gardening clothes. The legs of Mrs Rankin – like a centurion. Her habit of waggling a shoe from one fat toe. (Unaccountably sexy, this.)
- Charlie playing Mozart's *Rondo à la Turque* on his teeth, and my wife finding it hilarious.

Queen Mothaire?
..O, I think she eez about 96 years old ... ..she eez really a marvull, eezn't she?

TICKA TACKA TICKA TACKA TICKA TICKA TICKA TACKA

At this point I realised some of us were a bit drunk. Perhaps I was too, because I found myself asking Mrs Rankin her reasons for adoring living in France. All English people when I ask them, give the same reply, and it always enrages me.

THE FOOD...THE WINE...THE WEATHER... ...GORGEOUS COUNTRYSIDE.... ..DECENT ROADS
C'est tout?
mmn.. yes.

?
Mais, Madame!! What about US!?

NOUS.. nous les français!
You cannot 'ave France wizzout zer Franch peepoll!!
Ahlala! Raymond arrête!
Why are we not on your leest!? c'est MONSTRUEUX!

Don't you like Franch peepoll?..
Oh abs'lutely um, I mean...

I like French people!
!
O, Gemma! Hi, babes!

You like all of us... or just Hervé de Bressigny?
Bonsoir Madame
Bonsoir Madame!

Ooh Gemma! do I spy sushi?
Interesting to drink a Loire so old...
Yeah..sushi and sashimi

A note on Gemma's food:
It's prejudice, but one doesn't expect great things dining *chez les anglais* – I'd resigned my guts to some peasant mess to match the decor.
In fact Gemma had been quite extravagant. (Was I the only one to find it a little distasteful to sit in this pastiche of rural poverty eating *filet de boeuf* at 165 francs the kilo?) The wine (St Nicholas de Bourgeuil 1976) was excellent and the dinner was bizarre rather than bad. For example, why serve expensive fish raw? Why turn it into a plate of Lego?

Sea bass sashimi
mixed leaves
Brillat Savarin
Char-grilled Carpaccio with polenta wedges
Vodka, ginger & lime granita

If Gemma *had* committed adultery, she gave nothing away at dinner. There were none of the usual signs – no guilty over-attentiveness to her spouse; none of those smiles and blushes that arrive unbidden with some steamy recollection. No, Gemma wore her usual cool expression. (Fishes look at you with more animation.) I began to think I was wrong. Nothing had happened. She was probably a prude and, in any case, she didn't look the part of an adulteress – or certainly not the literary one I had in mind. (Exquisite, dark, refined, yet possessed of a fulminant sexuality.)

Really, your cottage eez ravishing!
Thank you
J'adore cette ambiance "cosy!"
...my kids..and English beer... that's all I miss living here...

Ooh YUM, Gemma!..I know this is good...it's a DELIA recipe, isn't it?...but where'd you get the mascarpone?..not in Bailleville?
No. Got it in Rouen

This British Madame Bovery looked like some kitchen skivvy, with her greasy apron, the soles of her feet rather black, her face a little pink from the oven and the sweat glistening between her shoulder blades. (Actually, I like the shine of a woman's hot skin.)

On her arm I noticed two weeping insect bites... and on her neck...

Tiens! That's not a mosquito bite!

That's a LOVE BITE!!
Isn't it??

I mean, don't you find shopping here absolutely BLOODY HOPELESS?? So many things you can't get...decent balsamic, ..pecorino...bottarga...labneh... ...norimake...shisso leaf... I have to bring it ALL from England!

C'est bien ça!!

It was a lovebite! I was sure of it. Passion's Postmark. Passion with Hervé de Bressigny.

In her diary, Gemma writes: Around 4 went back to Rouen for white wine, cheeses – got Brillat Savarin in Leclerc, which is where I saw him. He didn't see me to begin with, but after a bit, I Knew he was following me. So, round about the yoghurts, I faced him, said bonjour – and he blushed!

Mm..vous êtes amateur de bon vin à ce que je vois....
I've got people coming to dinner
Ah bon
Well, no... not at all bon...
...it's people I don't really want to see... I must be MAD... spent a fortune and two days cooking
Mais pourquoi?
Dunno... just something to do I s'ppose
..And you...you come all the way to Rouen just to buy tinned cassoulet.... frozen pizza?
eerr oui... just somesing to do...

Turns out he's walled up revising for an exam, but gives himself 2 hour break everyday – shopping. And following women in supermarkets I said, but don't think he understood – his English is better than my French, but not much. Kept giving me this sexy look. Thought he was about to ask me for a date.... but then he said he had to split and off he went. Driving home, I didn't plan it.. I just did it. Saw the chateau, thought all the more the merrier, I'll invite him for a drink.. and belted up the drive. Got soaked on doorstep. After three rings was going to call it a day.

?

...fait chier... qui vient m'emmerder?...

Rrring

J'arrive J'arrive!

!!

Hi!

He did let me in the hall – HAD to because of the rain – but I got a very small hallo. He seemed v. twitchy, embarrassed. Anyway, I asked if he wanted to come round for a drink. Said no, he couldn't – but in off-hand way. So I thought Sod you, I'm off. Then thought before I went I'd grab a quick look at the château – seen it often enough from the road.

Was like I'd asked to see his bank account – he seemed really pissed off, said something like it wasn't convenient. Anyway, was allowed to see one v. dark passage, smelling of churches.. and two rooms. (From Gemma's diary)

* c'est un vrai taudis... je n'ai pas besoin de tes réflexions sarcastiques

* HOUSE IS IN CRAP ORDER... I CAN DO WITHOUT YOU SNEERING AT IT.

House isn't much to write home about – Victorian pretending to be 18th century – rather boring EXCEPT it's in the most WONDERFUL state of decay. Everything's completely knackered – bald rugs, damask and brocade in shreds... anything wood is riddled with worm... everything faded to elephant's breath colour. TOTALLY STUNNING!

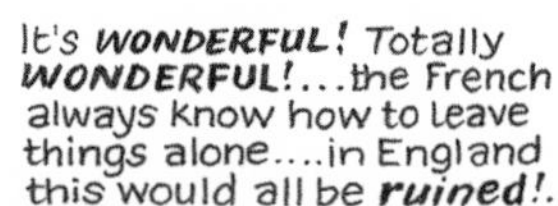

It's **WONDERFUL!** Totally **WONDERFUL!**...the French always know how to leave things alone....in England this would all be ***ruined!***...

?

... be all smothered in National Trust paint.....ponced up.... chintzed up... festooned to buggery....
??

See, you can't **make** an atmosphere like this – it's the **REAL THING**... **REAL** decay...real ruined grandeur Don't ever touch it! It's **WONDERFUL!!**
Wondairfool? Ah bon?

I was just thinking, actually the panelling would look really amazing stripped... when there was this massive great clap of thunder...

KhABBBBOOMM!!
!
!
Bloody hell!
That's close!

Crrakk!
Drrinng...
...Drrinng...
Drrinng....
Drrinng
9!!
Hervé! Mais qu'est ce que tu fais?....Tu viens de courir?...Alors, tu as bien travaillé aujourdhui?*
Uhhn... Oui, maman...
* WHAT'RE YOU DOING? HAVE YOU BEEN RUNNING? HAVE YOU DONE SOME WORK TODAY?

(From Gemma's diary)

Still can't quite believe it happened – didn't plan it that way. Very sudden. Very rash. On the other hand bit of a buzz. Of course, now I worry about the furniture. We fell on stool and chair thing with terrific whumph. Dust every-where. Knew something went. Had a look later. Underside full of worm. Some new. Couldn't see any break. 19th century I think. Carpet certainly Aubusson. V dusty too.

For the rest of the evening I remember sitting there almost hugging myself. Madame Bovery had a lover, just like the book! I thought it so amusing, fool that I was.

I awarded myself first prize for observation. That lovebite on her neck – one just knew it couldn't be Charlie's doing. No, it was Hervé. The little brute got carried away.

It was strange how that crass little mark changed one's perception. How, like a seal of approval, it seemed to make Gemma more . . . covetable. And her expression, which one had read as polite *ennui*, now struck me as signifying robotic self-control. She gave nothing away. Occasionally she blinked. Once or twice her mouth opened in a tiny gasp.

C'était magnifique.

Ah...perhaps Madame will know....
Yes, Gemma... you're the gardener... what would you put against a north-facing wall..?
erm...
Tu dois rester! Don't go! c'est pas possible!
I must!.. I've got people coming at 8·00...
Alors, on se voit demain, n'est-ce pas?
Tomorrow?..uh...dunno... Depends. I might do.... if... that is...
Listen...this is just fun..OK? nothing more..just fun...
Fern? Qu'est ceque c'est fern?
Amusement...bit of a laugh... I'm bored, you're bored...we just have fun, OK?
...and another thing... NO QUESTIONS..you know I'm married and that's all you need to know...
..and I don't want to know ANYTHING about your love-life
Comment?
said I don't want to know about your girl friend...
Delphine!
Cheers all!
Night Night
Merci, Charlie ...c'était fort sympathique
Merci Madame c'était une soirée superbe!
Good night...

The next day was Sunday – one of my free Sundays when I didn't have to go to the bakery at dawn. I could have slept late but the Boverys' aperitif had given me a hangover so bad my hair hurt. At 6 am, unable to bear the loud crepitations of feathers in my pillow, I got up and went out. In fact, I took some rubbish to the bin in the lane, which was where I heard a smoker's cough – not the full tar-box kind like mine, more a cadet version.

Hervé looked mad, I remember, grinning and grimacing.

Tiens!... Hervé de Bressigny!

* Mais qu'est-ce que j'ai fait..? Je ne peux pas la voir...
*I'M MAD! BLOODY MAD ...WHY'D I DO IT ??!!! I CAN'T SEE HER AGAIN I CAN'T!! I CAN'T! I MUST WORK! I MUST WORK! CAN'T SEE HER TODAY.. I CAN'T

* j'ai trop de boulot
une femme mariée!
très sexy
*
SOMEONE'D SEE HER... COMING TO THE HOUSE... MAMAN'D GET TO HEAR... ASK QUESTIONS... ...CAN HARDLY TELL HER WAS FOREIGNER I MET IN THE SUPERMARKET

* Je suis cuit si Delphine....
*
AND DELPHINE!! SHE'D FIND OUT! SHE FINDS OUT EVERY THING! SHE'D KILL ME ******* KILL ME!!! AND GEMMA'S HUSBAND AGHh! I MUST NOT SEE HER AGAIN.. TELL HER SORRY, BUT NON!.. I WON'T ANSWER THE DOOR...PRETEND I'M OUT...

It wasn't hard to guess what had brought Hervé almost to Gemma Bovery's gate. Lust, and curiosity to see where she lived. But then he uttered, or rather groaned, the name Delphine. Delphine?? So bonded in my mind was Hervé with Gemma, I'd overlooked the idea of his already having a girlfriend.
But of course he had. A smart one, according to my niece, Crystelle, my best informant on events at the chateau. Delphine was 21, Parisienne, with her own studio flat in a snob *quartier*. She was dabbling in a course at the Mécénat d'Art and was thought by Hervé's mother to be almost perfect daughter-in-law material. Delphine's lineage was disappointingly bourgeois, but her papa was rich and, the talk was, she'd bring enough to a marriage to re-roof La Boissière several times.
There's no way of knowing how much Hervé loved her. Certainly, saying her name seemed to stop him in his tracks and make him turn abruptly, up a path which leads to the chateau.

My sighting of Hervé was, I believe, coincidence. Not so, my next glimpse of Gemma. Around five o'clock, I happened to be picking beans in my garden, and chanced to look up as a figure with pale hair swiped past my gateway, right to left. I arrived at the gate just in time to see Gemma disappear up the path Hervé had taken that morning. Of course, I didn't go back to picking beans.

!

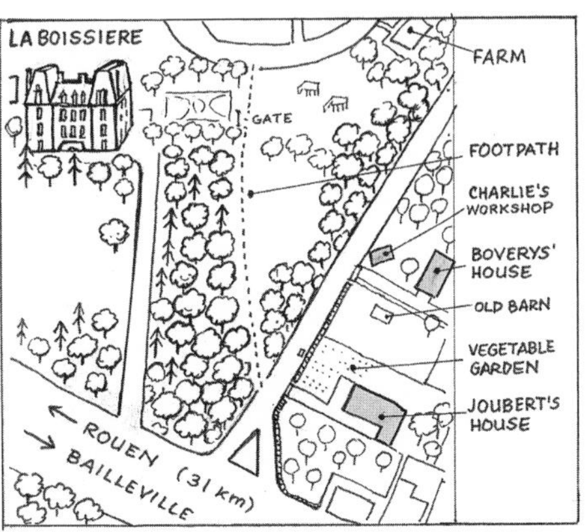
LA BOISSIERE
GATE
FARM
FOOTPATH
CHARLIE'S WORKSHOP
BOVERYS' HOUSE
OLD BARN
VEGETABLE GARDEN
JOUBERT'S HOUSE
ROUEN (31 km)
BAILLEVILLE

I went after Gemma, and if this sounds criminal – stalking a young woman – I can only protest that at the time it seemed quite legitimate. That blond flash had been like a signal. Like a flash from a mirror, and the fact that I caught it went beyond coincidence, *non*? I felt in some strange way as if I'd been summoned.

I told myself the only reason I was following Mrs Bovery was to confirm my speculations about her and Hervé. It would be enough just to see them meet.

..enough just to see him open the door to her...

NOTHING more...

Après tout, je ne suis pas voyeur...

I'd assumed the chateau to be the likely rendezvous, and was expecting Gemma to turn off through a small gate which gave into the grounds. Imagine my panic when Hervé loomed out of the bushes just in front of me.

Je suis désolé! C'est impossible! Il faut que je rentre à Paris tout de suite...je suis vraiment désolé...
Sorry, what's all that?

What did you say?
!

Say it in English..

...what were you saying..?

uhh... Rien...

Unhh!
Anh!

Let's go in the house

In the house..vite!

Peuff!
belle parti de jambes en l'air..

* TSK!...JUST A CRUDE BIT OF LEGOVER...AS ONE MIGHT EXPECT...

au romantisme du 19ième siècle...
les jeunes connaissent du romantisme?..
fièvres de l'anticipation..? *

* HARD TO IMAGINE **THEM** HAVING AN EXTENDED 19TH CENTURY-STYLE PASSION....I MEAN...

* **WHAT** DOES THEIR GENERATION CARE ABOUT **ROMANCE**? WHAT DO THEY KNOW ABOUT THE **CHASE**... THE FEVERS OF **ANTICIPATION**..?...

...de l'éxquis délice du plaisir différé...
...tous ces longs voyages de la découverte de la sensualité...

*....THE EXQUISITE SAVOUR OF DEFERRED PLEASURE...?

...THOSE LONG VOYAGES OF SENSUAL DISCOVERY...?

....ils ne recherchent que le plaisir immédiat!

* THESE DAYS IT'S ALL INSTANT SELF-GRATIFICATION! THEY CAN'T WAIT! THEY WANT EVERYTHING ***NOW!***

C'est l'érotisme fast-food!
On n'envie pas leur vie sexuelle....

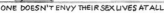

ONE DOESN'T ENVY THEIR SEX LIVES AT ALL

Ah..Tu es allé faire une promenade...bizarre..tu n'as pas emmené le chien...

AH..YOU WENT FOR A WALK?... FUNNY YOU DIDN'T TAKE THE DOG.

By the fifth day of Gemma and Hervé's liaison I remember thinking *ça suffit*! I didn't know why, but it really depressed me, I couldn't stand to see her disappear up the track to the chateau. I had a strange pang, as if a tiny rodent was gnawing my diaphragm.

Chomp

Was it because it seemed such a cold-blooded business? Was it the chewing gum? Was it the track suit? I mean, really! A French woman for a *rendez-vous d'amour* makes herself a little perfumed, a little sexy, *non*? But Gemma, she might have been going to rub down a horse.

I turn to her diary, where one might expect everywhere to see her lover's name and to find a confession or at least a debriefing of the day's romantic activity.

It's her husband she writes about most of all: how, shut away in his workshop, Charlie never notices her absences. Consequently, she never has to tell him lies. When she returns from her trysts she feels quite fond of him, feels like doing something to please him, "I made him bubble and squeak," she writes cryptically. She also feels so energised she wants to please other people. Even Wizzy Rankin, for whom at the *manoir* she carries out several decorative commissions.

Mural for Guestroom
£500 (cheque)

Punch'n'Judy cabinet
for children's bathroom
850 francs (cash)

Pasta Table Topiary
£25 (cash)

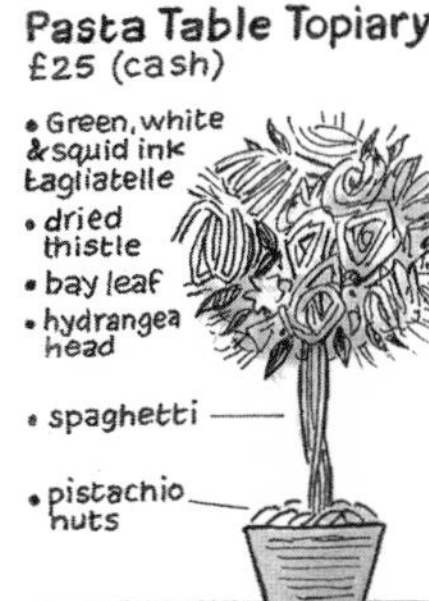
• Green, white & squid ink tagliatelle
• dried thistle
• bay leaf
• hydrangea head
• spaghetti
• pistachio nuts

Mm
God, Gemma, you're a STAR! You can make anything, can't you!

Of Hervé she writes only this: *Still don't know much about him – nor he me, beyond where I live & my name – or rather, my maiden name. Thought it safer... he thinks I'm Mme Tate. It's great not talking – no lies, no stupid things to regret saying. We meet, we collapse on the carpet & it's fantastic!*

I, Joubert, can hardly bear to read this now. At the time I was merely impatient for the grubby little business to end – as end it would, as soon as Hervé went back to Paris. A holiday shag with a married *anglaise* would be something he'd want to draw a line under, something to crow over with his *copains*. But something also to feel a little soiled by, something he wouldn't care his girlfriend to discover.

The next morning Hervé came into the shop . . .

. . . and bought two *pains au chocolat*. Very casually I remarked how time flew, September already. Wouldn't be long before he had to get back to Paris, *non*? Obligingly, he revealed he was on his way there now.

Ah, déjà sur le depart?

Alors bonne route! .... au revoir!
Merci
Au revoir

Allez, vas-y petit con!... Bon débarras!

*OFF YOU GO, YOU LITTLE TICK.... THAT'S THAT...END OF ROMANCE

Her lover had disappeared to Paris. Her brief affair was over. One might have expected Mrs Bovery to sink into the most profound *ennui*. But she didn't.

..et ça va bien aujourd'hui ?
oh oui..traytray bien!

Whenever I saw her she seemed to radiate rude energy, a kind of half-suppressed excitement. She told me that she was working hard, and her diary bears this out. It was a period of industry and earning: £3000 for illustrating *Follies and Monuments of Mood,* about £500 (cash) for stencils in Mrs Rankin's kitchen.

More importantly, this was a period when Gemma went shopping. Not in her usual manner. This was no longer a modest activity governed by economy and restraint but something frenzied, ravenous and entirely immoderate. A quite reckless scale of spending. Gemma writes that she hadn't had such a good shop in years. She'd quite forgotten what it was like.

Lingerie
AGNES
BARCLAYCARD
VISA
La Brocanterie
Antiquités

Among the things she bought in Bailleville, Rouen and elsewhere, she mentions: a sofa (15,000 francs), a screen (5,400 francs), two chairs, a staple gun, a marble pedestal, a book on Swedish Gustavian design, a quantity of antique *toile de Jouy* and other *tissus*.

Soon afterwards Gemma cleared her salon of its contents. *Le style agripauvre* – the lambing chair, the milking stools, the peasant chattels, the flail, the gelding irons – could be seen one Sunday afternoon assembled on the grass. By the evening they were exiled to the barn. The new decor (curtains, upholstery, covers and bed-hangings) she made and installed while Charlie was away in England.

Gemma described it as "sort of Swedish Dangerous Liaisons."

Sitting room: white linen; Toile de Jouy, pink madder on white – for cushion & screen.
Spare Room: Grey & white linen

Beauté tonic

..et c'est enrichi en nanocapsules de Vitamine E... c'est un effet "Lissage"..
Visag

Madame Bovery had also been refurbishing herself. "Props," she called them, the boots, shoes, belts, stockings, make-up, the long dark cashmere coat and hot water bottle. Reading her diary one has the impression of her preparing for a role, as an actress does, practising certain gestures and *maquillage*, learning how to comport herself in unfamiliar dress.
Was Charlie aware, one wonders, of the afternooons she spent in her bedroom "putting on slap and perfecting the overcoat drill." She adds, "There's no point in not doing things properly."

marisa
Hii...Good time in Rouen?

In public Gemma's appearance seemed unchanged. When she came into the shop she looked as slovenly as ever. But then one would be struck by some new and incongruous detail. Lipstick, for instance, one day. The next, mascara. Another day, high heels – things I'd never seen her wearing before.

Then, one day in October, she appeared in full costume, and I realised she was trying to play that most banal of characters – *la blonde* – which is of course not a character, merely a tired arrangement of characteristics. Don't young women realise how utterly bankrupt that image is? It's the currency of 40 years ago, of their mothers' youth.

!

That bleached fringe.
The stupid little nose.
The hard eyes.
The sulky mouth.
The silly little skirt.
The erect ankle and extended leg – which in Nature, in certain deer, for example, is the signal of sexual availability.

Really one had to yawn.
I found her quite without allure.

et voilà 3 croissants, 3 brioches...
ay une tarte aux pommes

c'est tout, Madame?
...erm..no... un baguette s'il vous plaît

..et votre mari... il va bien?
oh oui tray bien

She'd been gone three minutes when we discovered her bag of croissants on the counter.
My wife suggested I deliver them to the Boverys on my way home.
As I strolled up the path I noticed that Charlie's van wasn't there.
The lights were on, and in spite of the closed windows
there was a roar of opera (Mozart).
I knocked. I called. I tapped on the glass.
Nobody could hear. Not
even the dog, Carrington.

Dove sono i bei momenti

!

Total transformation! The shepherd's chair, all the swarthy rusticana, had gone. In their place, pallor – a decor of white and pale grey.

Two figures moved into my line of vision. Moved out of it, then in again and finally disappeared. Gemma and Hervé de Bressigny.

tu es sûre pour ton mari?

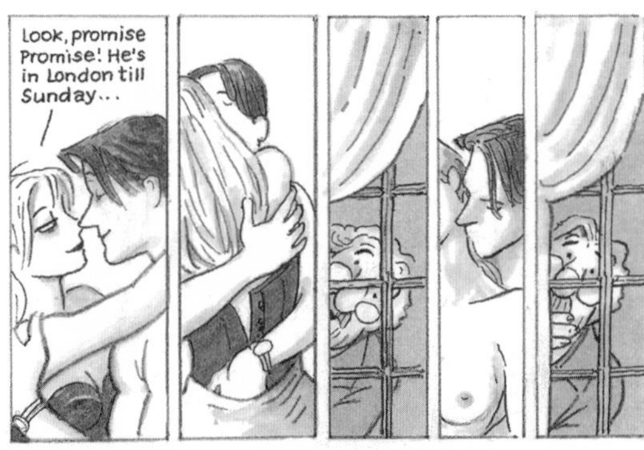
Look, promise Promise! He's in London till Sunday...

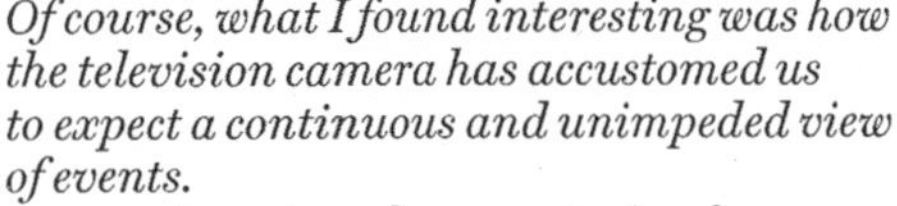

Of course, what I found interesting was how the television camera has accustomed us to expect a continuous and unimpeded view of events.
I mean, in nature documentaries, for example, when a snake follows a rat down a hole, the camera goes down too. Preceding the reptile, it permits us, the viewer, to wait with the anguished rodent, in what soon becomes une petite chambre épouvante, *a little chamber of horrors.*
But thankfully, in real life when a rat and a snake disappear into the ground, c'est tout! *We see nothing else. They leave us outside the hole and spare us the sight of something a little appalling.*

This is what I felt when Gemma and Hervé disappeared.
I walked home in the dusk. With Madame Bovery's breakfast undelivered.

Gemma writes: It was mega. In our spare room. We talked a bit this time - rationed each other to two questions. Asked him his age & if he'd passed his retake. He has - is now in degree year - which I thought makes him a baby, about 22. But turns out he's older. Said he always made a muck of exams, was late getting his BAC, then did national service. He asked my age - was surprised. Also asked *exactly* where Charlie was. That's all. Think he also doesn't want to know too much. Sexier being strangers.

Relax! It's only the dog scratching!

I assumed he'd stay and drive back to Paris after breakfast - but he got more and more jumpy about Charlie suddenly coming back.

!?!
S'O.K! only MICE

Honestly! He's away till Sunday...

But.. I sink I go now
OK..as you like

Seemed like he couldn't get out of the place fast enough. Thought I'd blown it. Big turn-off inviting him here. But at front door he said next time it might be better to meet at the château - said he'd fax me when. So - he wants a next time.

Paris

RUE D'ASSAS
Ah elle est anglaise?
Ouais

She's 30! Married! Her house is full of mice! Hervé, you're MAD! ..t'es complètement givré!
Mais, elle est extra au lit...

But you're crazy!
I know... ...I can't help it

17e Arr
RUE MAURICE LENOIR
But, Hervé.. what're you saying?...

...you want to spend part of the term at La Boissière? Why? Why can't you work here?

It's just I can concentrate in Normandy, Maman... ..there're no distractions... ......I can do all my assignments there...
And what about your lectures, Hervé?

Oh, I'd be here for important ones. The rest - a friend's going to copy his notes for me... Arnaud

I just hope you know what you're doing...
..if you DARE to fail this summer, That's IT! I wash my hands of you! SICK of paying for you to mess about!

You haven't mentioned Delphine ...things are all right, are they?... because you won't see much of her if you're in the country.... What does she think about it?
She's fine
Ah. I'm very glad to hear it!

AVENUE MATIGNON
..Hervé, you can't be in Normandy then!..you'll miss Ségolène and Matthieu's party!
Mm

Tu m'écoutes, oui ou non!!?

You're so preoccupied all the time! Qu'est-ce que tu peux être casse-pieds avec ton travail!
Sorry, Delphine, I'm sorry!

To avoid questions, I lied about Madame Bovery's croissants.
I told Martine that they were safely delivered, when in fact I ate them on my way home.
Unfortunately Martine can often spot a lie.

What do I mean? I mean CRUMBS, Raymond..all over your beard... all over you!...Admit it, you ate them, didn't you!!?

You were just too bone idle to take them round! But it's dishonest!! She PAID for them... WHY did you do it? You're MAD!!

..tu perds la boule, ou quoi?

I was at a loss to explain. Nothing would make me tell her the real reason why I couldn't deliver them, nor what I'd seen through Gemma's window. It was just the sort of juicy item Martine loves passing on to customers. In no time it would have been all round Bailleville – an insupportable idea from my point of view.
You see, I wanted Gemma's secret to remain exclusively mine. I was like the leopard who stashes his kill – an antelope, perhaps – high in a tree, beyond the reach of scavengers.

The next afternoon, Martine announced with some animation that she'd just been round to the Boverys on her way home from the shop.
I was horrified, my imagination strewing Gemma's house with adulterous evidence – underwear, odd shoes, wine glasses, tumbled cushions. My wife feasting her eyes.
Thankfully, the details of her visit were rather different:

I took them a fresh bag of croissants – well it's only right, Raymond... ..naturally I didn't mention your stupidity to Charlie...

Charlie was there, wearing an apron.
He'd been in England for a week.
He'd just got back that afternoon with his children.
It was their half-term holiday.

Ah, how kind..ah, listen, sorry...I must just turn off something on the...
Come in!

Sorry..sorry..it's the kids' supper... ..Sorry, Gemma's upstairs on the phone...Have a glass of wine...
Ah! zer décor! all new!

Did I know, Martine went on, that English husbands do the shopping? Charlie had been to *supermarchés* both sides of the tunnel – in Ashford and in Calais. And English husbands don't sit around reading the paper, they cook the dinner. Proper *sauce bolognèse*.

Yes, Gemma redecorated while I was away.
She went MAD! God! What got into her...!?!

She spent a bloody FORTUNE we can't afford!

Yes..everything all white... does make it brighter..yes, she's clever like that...

And did I realise, Martine asked, that English husbands notice what their wives do?
Because while Charlie was away Gemma had changed all the decor in the salon as a surprise . . .
New furniture, paintwork, curtains, upholstery. All done herself! English husbands don't moan at the extravagance. They're really appreciative . . .

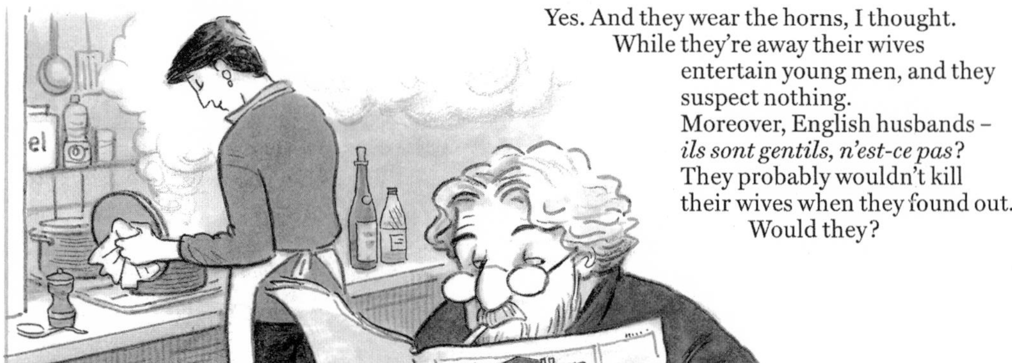

Yes. And they wear the horns, I thought.
While they're away their wives entertain young men, and they suspect nothing.
Moreover, English husbands – *ils sont gentils, n'est-ce pas*?
They probably wouldn't kill their wives when they found out.
Would they?

According to Gemma's diary "Affairs are absolutely O.K. as long as you don't get involved and you're really discreet."

Discreet, she and Hervé were. Probably I was the only person to know how often he came to Bailleville. When one walked by the chateau one saw his car parked sometimes for days at a time.

To my eyes of course, Gemma had adultery written all over her. It wasn't just the extra care she took with her appearance. To be even slightly in range was to find her irresistible. One couldn't help it. It was to feel the heat-seeking eyes, the smile, full beam, it was to feel oneself entering a particle storm of pheromones.

Bonjour, Gemma!
Hi!
Ça va bien?
Oh oui... tray bien

How can an affair be bad when it makes me feel so good? When it makes me want to make everyone feel good – esp. Charlie? I really get on with him these days I feel good, so he feels good so I feel even better. Funny how love rubs off.

True, Love did rub off. Gemma was so brimming with love that she took her stepchildren to Paris Disneyland – a half-term treat costing over £200. Love and Disneyland encouraged Delia and Justin to hold Gemma's hands for the first time ever – hot little clasps, making her, also for the first time, feel fond and maternal.

So fond and maternal that when she took them to Rouen, she bought Delia a coat and Justin some sport shoes.

This unexpected largesse made the children so enthusiastic about their stepmother when they got home to London, that it prompted Judi Bovery to send one of her letters.

A letter which Charlie, so cheered by Gemma's high spirits and her improved relations with his kids, was able to laugh at.

ROUEN
Val-de-Reuil
Gaillon
Vernon
Évreux
Mantes
Versailles
PARIS
Dreux
Disneyland Paris
PARIS
MARNE-LA-VALLÉE/CHESSY

you have never parented them consistently. both of you seem to think spending is a substitute for caring. Thank you encouraging their acquisitive appetites, satisfy even if I was stupid enough. now you plead so poor, even though huge disposable income Tax free??!!! Some of us have to our whack. Not a day goes by shopping you to The Inland

"Shop me to the Inland Revenue!!
HAAAA!

Bye, Charlie!...just taking Carrington for a walk...
Brrr!

She called them BLISS, those afternoons with Hervé making the dust fly in the salon. Bliss, because she proved that, with a bit of stage management, Life could be perfect. That the right setting, props, costume and lighting could turn a good performance into something magnificent.

Thus in Gemma's mind Bliss and Perfection were a mixture of everything voluptuous and French: the champagne and foie gras she brought with her; her underwear; his underwear; the battered formality of the room; the dim November light and all the ghostly greys of decaying silk and petit point, which made her feel as if she was in a *grisaille* painting, something eighteenth-century.

?
!

!

Yes, Gemma called it BLISS – her low-risk, business-like business, with its clockwatching and prophylactics, its limited investment of the heart, the utter banality of its black lace this and black rubber that.

I, Joubert, remember those afternoons which led up to Christmas, as UNSPEAKABLE. A travesty of love!

When I saw what I saw (and this, after all, was only a little more than, say, a 19th-century gardener would have seen), when I saw what I was able to see (the windows were very dirty), I felt ill. I felt a thudding in my ribs, a gnawing in my vitals. I felt a chill slowly creep up my trousers. I would linger in the gathering dusk until one or other of them, usually Hervé, remembered to draw the tattered drapes.

How I hated him. How I hated him.

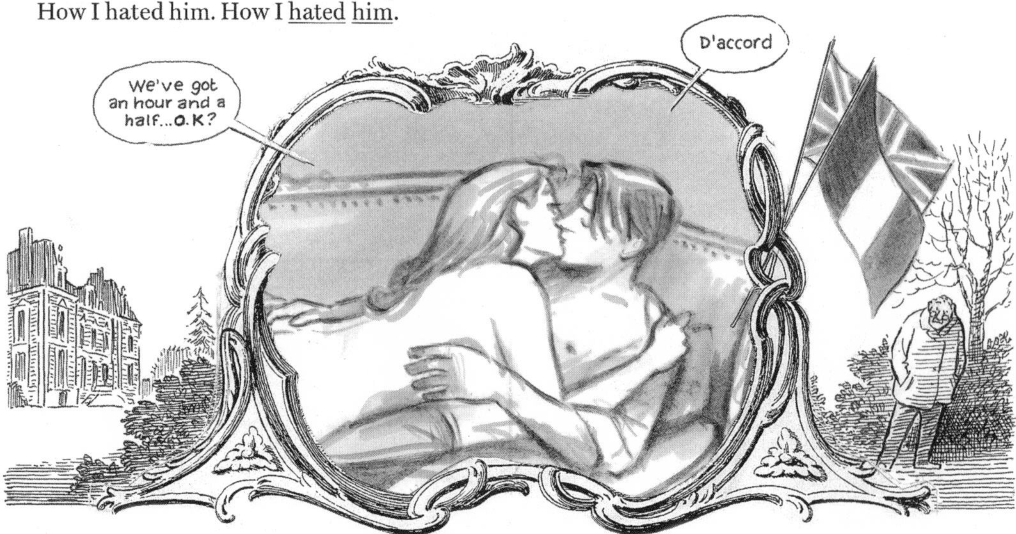
We've got an hour and a half...O.K?
D'accord

December 23rd (Hervé:) *Madame de Bressigny's goûter de famille rue Maurice-Lenoir, Paris XVII*

Elle est charmante * Delphine...tu ne trouves pas, Florence?
C'est regrettable elle n'a pas de **nom**... Bon, enfin ses parents ont l'air bien...

...et puis vous auriez vu la précédente.. **Sylvie**..son père était grossiste en salaisons... elle ***suait*** la vulgarité!.....

* She looks rather sweet, Delphine ... don't you think?
* Well, she's not **ONE OF US**...no name to speak of...however, her parents seem all right...and she's a huge improvement on Hervé's last one ...Sylvie...father was a meat wholesaler...She ***oozed*** vulgarity!

Salmon toasts
Dip
carrot batons
celery
cauliflorets
Brioches
fish pâté
Pâté de volaille
Champagne Moussant Tord-Boyau
Petits Fours
(frozen/from Picard Surgelé)

December 24th
(Gemma:)

Dec 24th Spent morning at the Rankins finishing their decorations - garlands, gilded artichokes etc. - bit of a waste as they're going back to England on the 27th. Wizzy paid me £100 cash - much needed. She treats me like hired help now and was pissed off when Mark asked Charlie & me to join the party this evening. We had caviar, blinis, sausage & mash - and wine costing a bomb. Apparently Mark's annual bonus is two million this year. He kept playing kneesies with me. Shut my eyes & thought of Hervé.

Chateau Latour 1970
... I'm going to get very, **VERY** cross in a..

In January Gemma's visits to the chateau began to last longer. Her diary records that afterwards, "talking" took place around the fire. She must have been aware that this was rash, because from the start she'd discouraged conversation. Intimacy was to remain purely physical. Anything else led to "promises, complications." Besides, she had found "sex with a stranger enough of a turn on."

Gemma and Hervé began asking each other stupidities – for instance, the four best things about France and England. Did they not realise that disclosure of trivia is the beginning of intimacy? And there is always the danger that the questions may become more personal and direct.

For France, I've got:
wine, food, countryside,
climate... you've got:
Culture, Paysage,
Vin, nourriture...

For England, I've got:
English Language, Gardens,
Pop music, London taxis.
You've got: Burberry
and Scotch whisky...
that's all

One afternoon Gemma had been examining the ceiling with its continents of water damage, years of stains that had come through three floors.

So, how much would it cost to mend your roof?
Des millions

Which your family hasn't got? Right?.....
Non

Where did your family's money come from...? Originally, I mean...

Eh?

What's the matter? ..is it that bad?

Hervé...Listen!...it's very usual.... In England, it's often something disgusting... like slaves...or

Eez not slaves!

C'était la quincaillerie en gros...au siècle dernier...
?

Look it up

Ironmongery...wholesale ironmongery..well, that's O.K. ...nothing wrong with that!

So they were sort of nouveau riche... ...how interesting!

And they bought their title.. How amazing!.... I always thought that The Revolution put a stop to all that stuff...but it went on in the nineteenth century, did it?

You're not listening, are you?
Non
...I 'ave a question for you..

Est-ce que tu...est-ce que tu couches avec ton mari en ce moment?
Do I sleep with Charlie?!

You really want to know?

On that afternoon I, Joubert, was taking my usual circular walk near the chateau.

!

I hate it that you sleep wiz your husband!

Je déteste que tu fasses ça!
But you do with whatshername, don't you?
Don't you?

No, stop! I'm not having this conversation..don't let's... Hervé..don't spoil...
NO!
TALK!

Why you stay with him eef you don't love him?... C'est dégoutant! Why don't you leave him?

None of your business.... We may or may not split up... I may or may not go back to England...
And you leave ME too...

It won't be like that, Hervé... It's nothing to do with leaving you! Listen, things like this don't last...YOU know that...
That's why it's so good..it doesn't last long enough to get...

Listen, in a month or two, you'll know I'm right...it won't be so exciting - it can't be! I'm only being realistic, that's all....

Je déteste la façon dont tu parles! ..the way you don't talk..of us... You are so cold! You don't feel! You feel nothing!...Rien! rien! ...je suis rien pour toi!

Hervé..listen, I've been really, really happy with you!

"'appy"??? MERDE!! Ecoute écoute Je t'aime!!
Je t'aime! Je t'aime! Je t'aime!
!

A demain...
tomorrow...

He loves me!!!

All I'd heard from that distance was Hervé's shouting he loved her. A little string of sound, but it cut through my heart like cheesewire. I remember feeling absolutely sick. You see, I already found their lust quite bad enough. Lust only claimed Gemma physically. But Love! I couldn't bear them to love each other. I couldn't stand for her to love him. Yet not five minutes ago, I'd watched Love transform Gemma and Hervé, had seen it change them from cool little fornicators into a pair of timeless *amoureux.*

Gemma went home where, according to her diary, she couldn't work, couldn't eat. At dinner while listening with half an ear to Charlie, she found herself crumbling bread into little balls and gazing at her reflection in the back of her spoon.

It's **bloody** Judi!! It has to be! She's bloody **shopped** me! Shopped me to the **Inland Revenue!!** **Dropped me** right in it! ...they want to see last year's accounts..**Aghh!** They're bound to look further back.....
Oh God! They'll really **do** me! I've had it!! **Bloody** Judi! How could she?? She always threatened to... thought she was joking..**how** could she **do** this to me!!??
Later on Gemma couldn't sleep. Never before had she encountered the full force of "Love – the L word." She felt on fire. She burned. Beside her Charlie lay in a cold sweat, with his own preoccupation – a letter from the English tax authorities demanding his presence in London.

And I, Joubert, lay sleepless too. The sensation I'd grown used to over many weeks, as if a tiny rodent lived in my diaphragm – had become insupportable! Now something immense – a beaver, a coypu surely, gnawed and gnawed at me. Only then was I able to identify this feeling: jealousy. Jealous love. I admitted it. I loved Gemma Bovery. I loved her! I hated her affair with Hervé de Bressigny.

It was then I decided it couldn't go on. Their relationship had to end. I had to destroy it!

So, how does one destroy someone else's love affair with a minimum of pain?
To begin with I tried thought transference.
This was not such a mad idea – after all, it had been my silent bidding which had caused Gemma and Hervé to meet in the first place. I had willed them to speak to each other, and they did so. I had willed them to have an affair, and they had. Now I willed their liaison to self-destruct. I seized every opportunity to deliver my subliminal message.

LEAVE HIM! Gemma, leave him!
...laisses le tomber, le petit con!..
...leave him!
Bonjour!
Une baguette
s'il vous plaît

The effect seemed to be the opposite. Almost every week Hervé drove down from Paris and he and Gemma grew bolder. They began to go out in public.
This was largely Gemma's idea. In her diary she says she wanted to know this young man who professed to love her. So she took him to lunch in Dieppe, Trouville, Honfleur – anywhere far enough away from Bailleville to soothe Hervé's fears of being seen.
Because he was "very nervous," she writes, "he nearly died when Wizzy's nanny spotted us."
(Gemma herself seemed to have no fears about Charlie's discovering. She would tell him she was just going out. He would look up from his work, but he never asked questions.)
She describes the utter excitement of those lunches with Hervé. It's the first time they've been in each other's company where they've kept their clothes on for longer than five minutes. It makes them quite shy, as if they've just met.

Hi Nicole!
Hi Gimma!

Afterwards they would return to the chateau. What followed makes uncomfortable reading.
I have to be thankful not to have witnessed these occasions. Flu had made us short staffed at the bakery and various extra duties prevented my usual afternoon walks near the chateau. Only once or twice did I finish in time to see Gemma returning home in the dusk.

Anyway, it appears from the diary that ever since Hervé's declaration of love their congress had been quite violently passionate.
And this was how a Sèvres figurine of Cupid and Psyche, one of the few good pieces left in the chateau, got knocked over and damaged and how it came to be taken back to Gemma's house.

..the foot eez broke! merde! Elle me tue si elle le sait!...my mother weel keel me...!

But Hervé! my husband -he can mend it! He restores all kinds of things...

Don't worry...I'll be very discreet. I'll think of a way of asking him...I won't mention you.

Gemma! C'est finie!.... ...feeneshed now, ton amourette!..Leave him...

Ah, the irony! At the same moment I, Joubert, was attempting to destroy Gemma's love affair, she was constructing plans for its future – something she'd only just permitted herself to do.

F
D
E
C
B
A
Gemma Bovery Interiors

Only now, reading her diary, do I realise how much Hervé's declaration of love had affected her. First, it made her spend money on him: restaurant meals, *un pull en cachemire*, a smart lamp for his desk, the dirty weekend she plans in London at Easter. Second, it stunned her, flattered her, excited her. It made her neglect her work, forget to return calls and open mail. In short, it made her a little crazy.
Third, it made her dream – pages and pages in her journal of elaborate fantasy – a soaring edifice that she built containing the following (and I summarize):

A. The business Gemma will set up in France. She adores France. "It is the only possible existence."

B. In the background, Charlie. Sometimes divorced from her, sometimes not. Her aimiable companion and business partner.

C. In her bed, Hervé. Gemma is not so crazy that she imagines marrying him. She realises that he will marry someone from his own background. But marriage does not alter their relationship. She knows the French to be "highly civilized about having lovers. Everyone has them." She receives Hervé like an 18th-century mistress, in a small pavilion, a place "brilliant for parties and for people staying."

D. Hervé's mother, Madame de Bressigny. A woman Gemma has never met, but who, after their introduction, commissions Gemma to redecorate the salon at La Boissière (three shades of grey over white) and the *salle à manger*, lacquered in *sang de boeuf*.

E. Clients. Friends and acquaintances of Madame de Bressigny, whose enthusiasm for Gemma's work has spread her name throughout the *beaux quartiers* of Paris.

F. Gemma and Hervé's love-child.

...I don't think I'd
want to get married
again...but I've often
thought of having a
child...just one...I'd
bring it up on my
own, of course...
!

Paris Delphine's car
..en bleu ou en rouge..and it comes in pale green, too...

Which d'you think I should get, Hervé?

Come on, you'll think of an excuse...

I've booked the hotel now..so you **have** to come... s'only a weekend!

It's so painless on Eurostar ...promise... and I'll come and meet you at Waterloo...
You're not listening are you?

But my examens... I'ave to study
Only three days away Herve... only three days....

Have you thought any more about my meeting your mum? See, I'm **sure** she'd like the panelling done....Supposing I did a bit to show her...restore one of these painted ones...see, I can pastiche ***anything!*****.....**

...I can do fake marble, porphyry, tortoise-shell...I could do a lovely bit of green and white **chinoiserie** in the little salon... You **HAVE** to introduce me, Hervé ..because she'd be so **useful**— She'd know ***masses*** of people with big houses like yours, who'd need stuff restored.....

Merde! How've I got myself in this ?!?
Hervé!

Who is she??!!
Il y a un autre dans ta vie...je le sens! There is someone!... I've known for weeks ....you do such different things in bed...you never talk to me any more...!
Mais dis-moi qui c'est!! mais DIS-MOI!

The "dirty" weekend Gemma arranged was fast approaching: three nights in a London hotel; Hervé to travel via Eurostar from Paris; Gemma *en voiture* via Calais and Dover. The (true) cover story she gave to Charlie was a meeting at Octagon Press to commission Gemma's illustrations for *Your Kitchen Garden.* She would stay with their lodger in the flat in Hackney. Of course all these details I have just learned from her diary. At the time all I knew for certain was that she was going to London – as she sometimes did. That Hervé would be with her was only a dreadful feeling in my guts.

eurostar

What gave me this feeling? I remember it well, I was in the pharmacy where my cousin Jeanne works. I was getting a cold which, when I saw Gemma, became positively a fever. She had that effect on me. I palpitated.

I noticed there were very blond streaks in her hair. She wore full make-up and a new black leather jacket. From the doorway, I heard my cousin ask Gemma if she was going on holiday – all her purchases, shampooing, dentifrice and so on were travel size.

Voilà Raymond: Aspirine...
...Broncolar...Balso Fumine...
...Biquinol...
c'est tout?

Non.non..juste à Londres... for my work..
Ah bon

Caisse d'Epargne Ecure

She's going with Hervé!!

I walked home, and as I turned into the lane Charlie Bovery and one of his children (it was their Easter holiday) came out of my gateway. Poor Charlie, he looked so depressed. Did he know about Gemma's affair? My wife told me he'd called in for help with some letters or bills – he couldn't understand the French. But I hardly took it in. I could think of nothing but Gemma.

Unpaid bills...telephone...electricity
His wife pays them..but she forgot...
I said, if you're not quick about it, they'll cut you off...

GEMMA!!
Gemma Bovery!

I wish I could say that what I resolved to do next – to utterly smash the romance between Gemma and Hervé – I wish I could say I did it out of male solidarity with Charlie. But he had nothing to do with it. If he'd looked distraught that afternoon, then I was a thousand times worse. His wife was driving me mad! She was in my head, in my belly, not for one moment could I stop thinking about her.
I remember standing in the orchard in a blur of pink and white and at my feet the lusty new grass, acid green, the green of bile, the green of Jealousy. I knew what I had to do. I went immediately to my study and seized the weapon, a new copy of *Madame Bovary*.

GUSTAVE FLAUBERT
MADAME BOVARY

I sent Gemma an envelope. As soon as it disappeared in the box, I remember feeling a rush of self-disgust. I couldn't believe myself, to sink so low as to send anonymous mail. Now, reading her account of how she received it, I feel even worse. It was not only base, it was cruel, indefensible.

When the *poste* arrived Gemma was upstairs preparing for her adulterous weekend, cutting little plastic tags out of new lingerie. In an hour she would leave for Calais. By the end of the day she would be in London with Hervé.
That she had misgivings about the trip is clear from her diary of the day before.

Three nights together - maybe it's a mistake. Just too much - we might not get on.. might run out of things to say. I so want it to be a Love thing but maybe it is just a BED thing. I'm such a fool, it was perfect. Should've left it as it was. Terrified now I'll screw it up.

Thanks Justin...

Anh!

Had to lock myself in the bathroom - Justin's always so nosy about letters. I had a really terrible feeling about it. Address was typed in caps.. to Madame Bovery. Local postmark. Posted yesterday. Didn't want to open it

Inside she would have found two pages photocopied from an English translation of *Madame Bovary*, with several sentences marked in yellow highlighter. All from the letter Madame Bovary's lover sends her on the day of their elopement, ending it all.

Be brave, Emma, be brave! I do not want to ruin your life ....
...... Believe me, I shall never forget you. I shall always be deeply devoted to you. But who can doubt that one day, sooner or later, these ardent feelings of ours would cool? We should have grown tired of one another...
.... I will be far away when you read these sad lines. I wanted to get away as soon as I could, so as not to be tempted to see you again...
.... Emma, forget me. Why did I have to know you? Why were you so beautiful?.................................
...............................Adieu. Adieu!.............

It's a joke..don't BELIEVE it!..... Hervé... he wouldn't!.. not like this...he wouldn't!!

How DARE he!? How dare he tell me like this!!?.... ...DUMP me! Dump me like this..!

Oh God ...is this the way they do it in France ?... ...so bloody cultured, they do it with literature!?

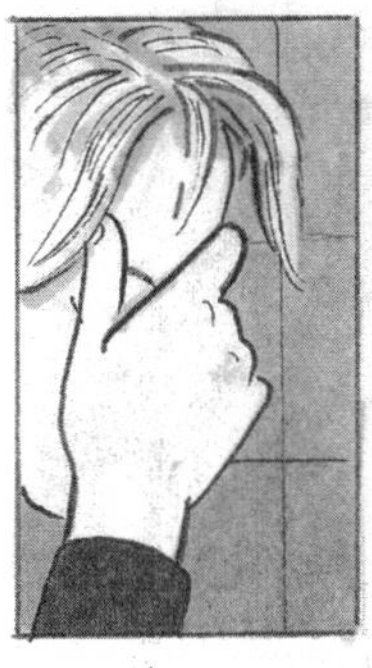

Autoroute service station 90 km from Paris

espace
communication
FAX
Mais vas-y!
Hervé!
FAIS-LE!!

Je ne peux pas!
DO IT!
Hervé,
DO IT!

DO IT! Before it's too late!

You're mad if you don't!
...think of Delphine...
Mais vas-y! Fais le!

Bailleville Normandy

In her diary, Gemma writes:

I was just thinking it might be OK after all – Hervé couldn't have sent the anonymous stuff – it was addressed to Mme Bovery. Hervé only knows my maiden name. Was feeling slightly relieved. Till I heard the fax.

rRring!

dzzz...
dzz...dzzz

!

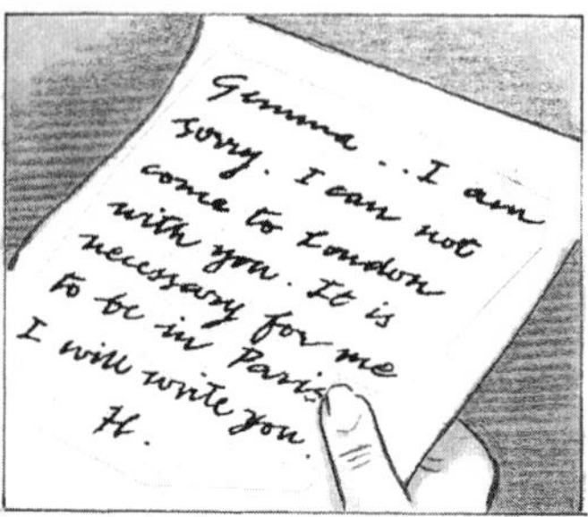
Gemma .. I am sorry. I can not come to London with you. It is necessary for me to be in Paris. I will write you.
H.

Second punch in the stomach. Worse. Everything very loud and clear. It's over, he's dumped me. Bastard. Wanted to die. The thought of having to carry out the charade and go to London was total nightmare – if it hadn't been for my meeting on Monday, would've stayed at home. Or would I? Could NOT have faced Charlie. Could hear him in the garden with Judi. Arguing as usual. She'd come to collect the kids on her way to Brittany.

OK.. how d'you explain it?... WHY did they choose ME to investigate?
I DUNNO!... your stuff came to the top of pile... anyway, if you're on the fiddle that's your look-out!

Charlie! I did NOT shop you! D'you think I'm that stupid?! Your financial mess is mine too

...I said... make a clean breast of it... underdeclaration.. Five years! TAX plus the interest plus a penalty £28,000!!
God! you've got it? What're we going to do

They always sound like they hate each other and I used to think they did. But really, their yelling's sort of game, sort of ritual. Judi makes Charlie come to life – he never rows with ME, never looks at me directly like that. Hardly reacts to me at all these days. Judi matters to him in a way I don't. They have a relationship – which I don't with anybody, any more. Watching them made me feel even more terrible. Made me want to get the hell out and never ever come back.

Gemma! What're you doing? You should be leaving... you'll miss the ferry!

GB

I, Joubert, knew Gemma went to London. I heard the van roar past my house.
I saw the dog Carrington come down the lane and stand
at the junction gazing mournfully after her mistress.
How I wanted to grill that small dog! If only it could talk.
I had so many questions. Did Gemma receive my envelope?
Did she think it was from her lover?
Did it plant in her mind suspicion? Doubt? Panic? Fear?
I asked myself, would it lead to a scene with Hervé?
Would it destroy their *affaire*? Or might it
have the opposite effect, and draw them
closer together?

Gemma was away five days. For my part, five days of tortured speculation. On the sixth day there she was, queuing in my shop. My heart lurched. I couldn't bear to look her in the eye. I turned my back, I trembled, fumbled, dropped coins. Martine served her.
What I did see told me that her *affaire* was over. It was obvious – the sad face, the lifeless eyes, the new *coiffure*. (I know from observing office romance that women always cut their hair when crossed in love.) If I needed other proof, there was the continued absence of Hervé's car under the lime trees at La Boissière. And when she went for a walk she went straight past the chateau with her head bowed.

I remember feeling a moment of triumph, a moment relishing my cleverness – how very fitting it was that two pages of *Madame Bovary* should end the love affair of Mrs Bovery. But it was only a moment. The truth was that I was not only appalled at this turn of events, but also fearful of the strange influence I seemed to have over Gemma's life. I had no sooner invoked the story of Emma Bovary for Gemma's behaviour to take a parallel course. Her actions seemed to follow the plot. Very amusing to begin with, but then, when I considered how the book ends, alarming. As everyone knows, *Madame Bovary* is a tragedy. It's not just love affairs, it's debt, scandal, arsenic, the heroine's agonising death.

People might have considered me mad then, to fear that tragedy might also overtake Gemma. Could I not have reassured myself that every day in Normandy countless women cheat on dull husbands without eating rat poison?

I resolved to do two things. First, to stifle all thoughts of Flaubert's novel. Second, to end my foolish obsession with Gemma. I knew I was incapable of not seeing her, but I decided to keep my distance, a distance I would make a little greater every day in the hope that slowly she would become an indistinct and remote figure. When I saw her I would think of something pure and peaceful. I would think of my dough resting for its second time, the long breads lying on their *couche* of floured linen and in their wicker *paniers*,
the pretty rounded *boules*, emitting that sharp,
heady little odour of fermentation.

Paris

Tu écris à Delphine?

Non. Delphine - c'est la cata...
She won't talk to me..she sent my letter back...no, I'm trying to write to Gemma...
Gemma!?

I **have** to write to her, Arnaud...
I thought you'd finished with her! You're **mad**, Hervé!..

I'd forgotten... She's got this statuette of ours... ***valuable*** one. It got damaged and she was going to get her husband to mend it. Trouble is, my mother's going to Normandy soon - she's bound to notice it's not there! ***She'll go spare!***...I've ***got*** to get it back from Gemma before then!
Well, **FAX** Gemma! Dont write flowery letters... You'll only encourage her. She's a disaster...

No, Arnaud, you're wrong... in many ways she was perfect...

I think she deserves a letter...

Bailleville Two days later

* Chère Gemma

Tu avais raison quand tu disais que le bonheur ne peut durer éternellement. J'aurais tant voulu que nous puissions continuer à vivre ces moments heureux, mais il faut se résoudre à accepter la réalité.

Je garderai toujours le souvenir de ces instants précieux que nous avons passés ensemble. Je ne t'oublierai jamais.

Je t'embrasse

Hervé

P.S. Concernant la statue ... vres
pourrais-tu me faire ... elle
a été réparée: tu peux lai...
message chez mon ami ...
au numéro suivant 01 46 ...
Même si elle n'est pas ré...
faut absolument que ...
passer pour la ...
Merci d'avance.

Gemma's diary

Today letter came from Hervé - addressed to Mme Tate. Forget he doesn't know my married name. Charlie remarked on the envelope, asked who it was from. I had to create a diversion, pretended wasp was in my hair. But really I wanted Charlie to know who it was from. Now it's over between me and H, I'm so sick of keeping it a secret.

Never thought he'd write - give him marks for that. And good there were no apologies, explanations etc. Couldn't have stood them. Know it must've been something to do with Delphine.

V. short letter. Everything sounds better in French.

I'd completely forgotten about H's bloody statuette - still shoved in the drawer with my tights. Never found the right moment to ask Charlie.

As H. has taken his time to write, think I'll take my time to reply. Let him sweat a bit.

*You were right when you said that happiness can't last for ever.
I wanted it to go on and on, but we had to accept reality.
I shall always treasure the memory of our time together.
I will never forget you.
P.S. About the Sèvres figure. Could you let me know if it has been mended? You can leave a message on my friend Arnaud's number. Even if it hasn't been mended, I really must have it back. Thanks.

La Boissière

Bailleville

Hervé?... écoute... I don't think we've been burgled..but..

..but one of the Sèvres figurines is missing... "Cupid & Psyche"... You didn't move it, did you?

Chipped? How?..you don't know?....So where is it?... Where!?? You gave it to whom?...un anglais??
Hervé! Whatever possessed you?? ..it needs a specialist!.....No, it can't wait for you to sort out... Where do I find this monsieur?

...WHERE?..Stop mumbling Hervé!... I take it this person is a professional restorer.....?.... WHAT? What d'you mean, you THINK so!!?

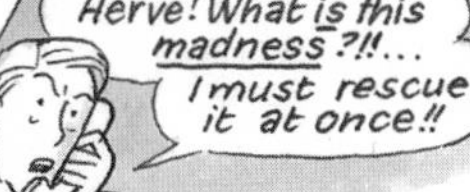
Hervé! What is this madness?!!... I must rescue it at once!!

Uhhh... je suis vraiment dans la merde...

Hi, there!
Bonjour monsieur... Je cherche monsieur Tate...

Tate?..ah, non! That's my wife...Je suis Charles Bovery...
Bovary?
Ah
?!
Florence de Bressigny ..Bonjour..

You speak French, yes? Now, I believe my son left a piece of damaged Sèvres in your care

Sèvres?..sorry? Pardon?

Yes, yes, Sèvres figures... en porcelaine... I hope you haven't done any work on it

...because, as I'm sure you appreciate, it's a valuable piece... I feel it really ought to be looked at by a conservator in Paris.

Sorry! Madame! Sorry, I don't understand!

Je sais rien de ça..O.K? I have no Sèvres..no porcelain I never met your son... I know Nothing! Rien! NIX!
!

Mais qu'est-ce que vous racontez, m'sieur! ...My son told me quite clearly he gave the piece to an anglais at this address... It must be you!...

Madam, you're mistaken! I know nothing about a piece of Sèvres.
Is there someone else here who...
My wife might know something... but she's out at the moment.

Monsieur Tate...this is a very worrying matter... I shall give you my card...this is my phone number...
Bovery!
Perhaps you would be good enough to ask your wife to telephone me in Paris?... I shall be returning there this evening.
Bien. Au revoir, m'sieur.
?

Paris

17e Arr
RUE MAURICE LENOIR
Your monsieur TATE, Hervé..a most repulsive anglais...in a VEST!
Un bonhomme vraiment antipathique!
He told me his name was Charles Bovary! ....not Tate
It's Tate, I'm sure

Of course it is! Why'd he give a false name?! Charles Bovary, indeed!

Anyway, Hervé..he said he never met you...he hasn't got our Sèvres..he denies ALL knowledge of it
How d'you explain this?

He did suggest his wife might know some-thing....

His wife?

Ah, his wife! Yes, yes of course! I completely forgot! She would know...

She really runs the business... Monsieur Tate, he just mends things... She said he was a bit up in the clouds... forgetful... doesn't concentrate... I remember it now...

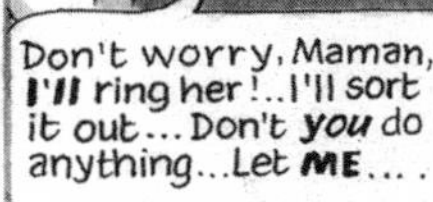
Don't worry, Maman, I'll ring her!..I'll sort it out... Don't you do anything...Let ME....

If it was Madame Tate you dealt with in the first place, why didn't you say so!!?
Where did you meet this woman, Hervé?..... Hervé! Answer me!
Uuh...Rouen...

Where in Rouen? Come on! Where?
uhh..in Leclerc
You mean to say you gave a valuable heirloom to a woman you met in the supermarket!! !??????

Have you gone MAD!! She's probably sold it by now!!

Maman! She wouldn't!! She mentioned her husband was a restorer...and..er...er.. I happened to notice the chipped foot on the figurine when I was in the salon...and so I thought..er...

You thought you'd give it to these peculiar foreigners-this so-called "Charles Bovary" & Madame Bovary, as I suppose she is! Really, Hervé!! ..She didn't come to the house... Did she?
No! I mean, yes... er...very, very briefly..just to inspect the damage...
...a minute literally...

And she went in the salon, did she, Hervé?
No. Um, well..just her nose round the door, perhaps
Her nose round the door. I see.

Thank you, Hervé...that explains the tray with the pâté, the cigarette ends, the two coffee cups I found shoved under one of the fauteuils..
...and perhaps it explains something else I found on the floor beside the chaise longue...

I'm disgusted with you!..C'est ignoble!! Tu me déçois beaucoup, Hervé! ...lies you've told... why you've been so keen to be here! instead of studying! ...how long's this been going on!?? ...married woman!! English!! how could you!? That's why Delphine won't see you?! Fool! losing her...

Well, you must tell this "Madame Bovary" that if she doesn't return the statuette immediately... I shall have to take legal steps...

(From Gemma's diary)

Found whole lot of letters today I never opened. It's awful, I just buried them. Both credit cards are in a lather – I've clocked up massive amount of interest without noticing. Am in a mess. Not much use telling Charlie – he's in much bigger mess. Tomorrow he goes to London to sort out some deal with the Tax Office. He's been a bit odd lately – he shaves every day & has had hair cut. Also he keeps looking at me, as if he's about to tell me something – and then doesn't.

What time you leaving?
Soon!

Gemma...does the name "de Bressigny" mean anything to you?
GUSTAVE FLAUBERT MADAME BOVARY

Uuh... no..... why?

A Madame de Bressigny came to see me the other day....

She said her son had given me a porcelain figure to mend...

..which was **news** to me...

She virtually accused me of lying... I was bloody annoyed!
Anyway...just thought I'd ask....

Charlie... listen... I... I may know something about it...the figurine ....it's in the chest of drawers ....

Listen..I want to talk to you...

I don't think you do, Gemma ...or, rather... I can guess what it's about...and I don't want to know.

Charlie!
Listen! will you please **listen!** I'm sorry, I...

GEMMA, I don't want to know! I don't want to know! O.K!
Look, I've got to go
Talk to me! Stop running away! **Talk** to me, Charlie!
Talk to you!?
Talk to you!
You've got a **nerve**! Months and months, you've done bugger all except waft around in a pink cloud... Don't think I haven't noticed! Now, suddenly, you want to talk!... I haven't time to talk!
When will you be back?
I don't know

Now it seems like one of those vanished summer months in a photo album.
But really it's only a short time ago, a matter of weeks, that I felt a sense of calm, of relief. Gemma's love affair with Hervé was over, and my own passion for her, stoked by jealousy and lust, which had roared inside me like a furnace, dwindled – to something like a pilot light. I felt almost normal. Once again I was absorbed and lulled by routine.
I rose early, helped make the dough, looked after the first *fournée* of bread; I served in the shop, chatted to customers, ate three good courses at one o'clock, napped, walked.

When I walked, I often saw Gemma Bovery in the distance. Although she made my heart pound, I was beginning to see her, too, as a creature of routine – an unexceptional young woman walking her dog.

She was of course a woman still not recovered from love. This is clear from her diary. She missed being loved. Missed sex. But she was sufficiently recovered to write that with Hervé "it wouldn't have worked," and that he was "the equivalent of a Hooray, someone I'd run a mile from in England, probably rather right wing." She thought his party trick – *faire la conchita* – an imitation of his mother's Spanish concierge, "a bit tacky."

I was musing about Gemma, of her resuming her bland life with Charlie, when I realised I hadn't seen him around for days. When I mentioned this to my wife (how she knew so much about it I don't know), she said Charlie'd gone to London. He'd got money troubles. Trouble with his tax affairs. He owed a lot. So did Gemma, come to that. On her credit cards. Debt, in other words.

It was the word Debt that undid my composure. Charlie's having debts was one thing, but Gemma having them was another matter. It meant that something sinister, something I'd felt to be contained, stoppered, had broken through the seal once more. A malign influence, a set of horrible coincidences, whatever it was, the curse of *Madame Bovary* – I was suddenly afraid that it hadn't finished with Gemma, that she was doomed to experience everything in the novel. But, I asked myself, did I really believe that she, like Emma Bovary, would kill herself? A bit of casual sex, a bit of overspending on one's Amex card, does that drive one to take arsenic? The idea was so mad, it's hard for me to explain why I feared it might be possible. Or not impossible.

I had been wondering how to discover the seriousness of Gemma's debt when, one evening, an opportunity presented itself outside my house. The dog Carrington had come into heat, had escaped and gone in search of love. It was I, Joubert, who saved her honour.

Fichez le camp
sales clébards !!

Carrington! You bad dog! O merci, Raymond.. thank you so much!

...um.. d'you have a minute?...
...I wonder if you would help me with something..?

mais... bien sûr!
?!
That's really kind of you...
Come in.. would you like a glass of wine?

I'd be **so** grateful if you could help me reply to it... I want to say something to shut them up while I try and sort things out – but my French isn't up to it...

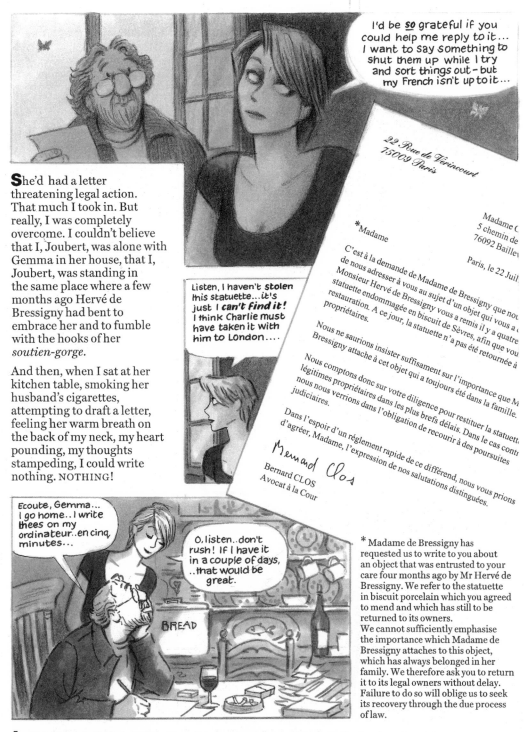

She'd had a letter threatening legal action. That much I took in. But really, I was completely overcome. I couldn't believe that I, Joubert, was alone with Gemma in her house, that I, Joubert, was standing in the same place where a few months ago Hervé de Bressigny had bent to embrace her and to fumble with the hooks of her *soutien-gorge*.

And then, when I sat at her kitchen table, smoking her husband's cigarettes, attempting to draft a letter, feeling her warm breath on the back of my neck, my heart pounding, my thoughts stampeding, I could write nothing. NOTHING!

Listen, I haven't **stolen** this statuette... it's just I ***can't find it!*** I think Charlie must have taken it with him to London....

22 Rue de Vérincourt
75009 Paris

Madame C
5 chemin de
76092 Baille

Paris, le 22 Juil

*Madame

C'est à la demande de Madame de Bressigny que nou
de nous adresser à vous au sujet d'un objet qui vous a
Monsieur Hervé de Bressigny vous a remis il y a quatre
statuette endommagée en biscuit de Sèvres, afin que vou
restauration. A ce jour, la statuette n'a pas été retournée à
propriétaires.

Nous ne saurions insister suffisament sur l'importance que M
Bressigny attache à cet objet qui a toujours été dans la famille.

Nous comptons donc sur votre diligence pour restituer la statuett
légitimes propriétaires dans les plus brefs délais. Dans le cas contr
nous nous verrions dans l'obligation de recourir à des poursuites
judiciaires.

Dans l'espoir d'un réglement rapide de ce différend, nous vous prions
d'agréer, Madame, l'expression de nos salutations distinguées.

Bernard Clos

Bernard CLOS
Avocat à la Cour

Ecoute, Gemma... I go home.. I write thees on my ordinateur..en cinq minutes...

O, listen..don't rush! If I have it in a couple of days, ..that would be great.

BREAD

* Madame de Bressigny has requested us to write to you about an object that was entrusted to your care four months ago by Mr Hervé de Bressigny. We refer to the statuette in biscuit porcelain which you agreed to mend and which has still to be returned to its owners.
We cannot sufficiently emphasise the importance which Madame de Bressigny attaches to this object, which has always belonged in her family. We therefore ask you to return it to its legal owners without delay. Failure to do so will oblige us to seek its recovery through the due process of law.

I told her I would certainly have written a masterpiece of prevarication in a day or two. As I got up to leave I remembered the question of Gemma having debts. Perhaps I was reminded by the pile of papers on the table. I could see bills from France Telecom and Electricité de France, and the distinctive envelopes of several registered letters. She must have followed my gaze, as she gave me a rueful smile, "Everyone's on my back at the moment," she said, adding quite cheerfully, "I'm just juggling with my credit cards.

At the door she asked when she should come and pick the letter up? Saturday? I said that I'd be in Rouen all day. (We sell our bread in the market.) Gemma said, "Oh, I go into town most Saturdays."

It's so clear to me now what I should have done. I should have told her to find me in the market and the transaction would have taken thirty seconds. But I couldn't help myself. I suggested a rendezvous around lunchtime. I would buy her a drink. "Where should we meet?" I asked, expecting her to name some café or brasserie.

La Cathédrale!?
I don't really know any cafés... if I'm in Rouen, I'll be in the **cathedral** about 12·30

I was taking a break on my threshold. Not an entirely relaxing five minutes. My head was still at work, honing and polishing the letter Gemma Bovery had asked me to concoct, when my concentration was pierced by the klaxon voice of Madame Rankin.

The sight of Madame Rankin is never unwelcome. When she's in residence in Bailleville she visits my shop twice a day. Her household eats huge amounts of bread and tarts of various kinds. Moreover, at the time I describe, she was preparing to celebrate her fortieth birthday with a large party. A marquee, and so on. Although the catering was being done by a Paris firm, she would come to me with a large and satisfying order. Only my bread would do at dinner.

I remarked her companion at once: an *anglais*, about 35, in breeding condition; an expensive linen jacket, his inside leg measurement much *en valeur*.

Boulangerie Joubert
She's talking lawyers now... she only lets me see Toby twice a week.. never on my own.. the nanny has to be there...
Oh NOOH! how ghastly! you poor thing!!

!
Gemma Tate? Oh yes, you said she lived here...

DID YOU KNOW HER HUSBAND'S JUST LEFT HER?
No, but then I barely knew she was married.

HER husband, Charlie - he's been doing my dining chairs.. looked a bit of a sad bunny - so I gave him a few Bloody Marys.... and he let it all out!

HE SAID GEMMA'D been having it off with some FROG!! Younger than her - our nanny saw him once. Anyway, MASSIVE BONKATHON all winter apparently!

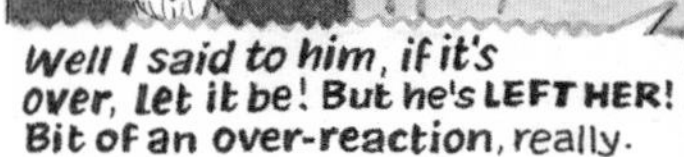

Well I said to him, if it's over, let it be! But he's LEFT HER! Bit of an over-reaction, really.

Now! this is the BAKERY I was telling you about

Bonjour, Ray! This is Patrick..he's a terrific fan of your bread! Il écrit sur nourriture en Angleterre... et il ADORE France
c'est vrai?

When foreigners speak of their passion for France, I can't help it, I always ask them their reason, as if it gives me pleasure to hear them reel it off in English or, more rarely, stammered in their imbecile French.

J'apprécie la France pour de multiples raisons: son vin, sa gastronomie.... ...ses paysages superbes... *

Mais ce qui est admirable, avant tout, ce sont les FRANCAIS... sans eux la France ne serait pas la France!

J'admire leur esprit, leur culture... ...et leur savoir-vivre

** Excusez mon français... il laisse à désirer...

All this was said with the most perfect French accent I have heard in a foreigner, accompanied with warm eye contact and the most winning of smiles. Absolutely repellent.

* I've many reasons for liking France: its wine, its food, its marvellous countryside, but what I find most admirable are the French themselves – their liveliness and wit, their culture, their savoir-vivre – without them France wouldn't be France.
** Excuse my appalling French.

(From Gemma's diary)

Thursday.
It's getting more and more serious. Today, horrible recorded delivery letter from the bank here – saying the cheque for electricity bounced again. So they've blocked my account for 12 months!!! Can't write any cheques. I must ask Joubert if this is normal practice. In England the bank's not nearly so hysterical – although am overdrawn there too. Nothing coming in till next month. Will have to ask Wizzy to advance cash for doing her book case.

Friday. Was over at Wizzy's. Asked her for a float – she said would a cheque do? Embarrassing having to say cash. She gave me 1000 francs in really patronising way. At least I can buy food and petrol.
Then I went in the sitting room and was doing the book case – when this voice goes:

Hallo, Gemma...
God!
Patrick!
✱?!✱! You gave me a fright!
What the ✱?!✱! are you doing here!?
Ah, good.. well, we seem to be on speaking terms...
Yeah... well I admit I was in the wrong, the last time we spoke
Patrick, WHAT are you doing here?
Staying with Mark and Wizzy
They were Pandora's friends... but they seem to have sided with me...
Oh. Didn't you know? Pandora kicked me out. I'm an orphan of the storm ..Wizzy's taken me in.
?

Pandora kicked him out! Couldn't help feeling gratified. He didn't say why, but I can guess. He came out with a lot of un-Patrick-like things – about having had a bad time, how he misses his son, how he's lost his licence for 12 months. While he's here, Wizzy's having to drive him everywhere.
Was I supposed to feel sorry? Don't know what I felt – I was in such a state at seeing him. It's all I need, him turning up like this. I have to work, I have to sort things out. I do NOT want to see him.
Fortunately, he's not staying very long – leaving after Wizzy's party.

You don't fancy driving me to the sea this afternoon, do you? Honfleur? Deauville?
No, Patrick, I don't. I've got work to do.
OK, not to worry
Anyway, France suits you, Gemma... I like the hair... you're looking very, very well...
O. bugger off Patrick

For two days I wrestled with indecision about my meeting with Gemma. Common Sense told me to ring up and pull out. Nothing good ever came from lunch with a married woman. As for the letter I had drafted for her – the reply to Madame de Bressigny's lawyer – I could just as well send it by mail.

"But," said another voice inside me, "Gemma needs you! She's in a mess, in debt, her husband's gone off. Over a drink, you can offer your help – to translate officious letters, to discover her liability for French tax, to sort out her finances. You can save her from ruin."

Then another voice, the voice of superstition screeched, "Don't ! Think where she's chosen to meet you. Rouen cathedral! It's the curse of *Madame Bovary* again. Think what happens in the book! Emma Bovary has a rendezvous in the cathedral. Immediately afterwards, in the course of an infamous carriage ride, she becomes Léon's mistress."

And yet another voice of mine sighed, "You mean, Gemma, my mistress? Well, I wouldn't mind, if it came to it. *Génial. Formidable!*"

Saturday arrived. Two hours before the arranged time I found myself in a phone box, primed to cancel the appointment. I composed Gemma's number, only to find that her line had been disconnected. I took this to be a sign. Fate wanted us to meet.

At 11.30, I left André at our stall in the market, saying I would not be back. I went to the barbers, had my beard trimmed, and a good splash of cologne, and just after midday, found myself outside the cathedral.

To pass the time I scrutinised the tourists. It seems that our era is the era of Shorts, the Era of the Arse. "Have we no shame?" I asked myself. And the answer was, "No." We all display our sub-standard buttocks and we don't care. Shame doesn't exist any more.

This led me back to Gemma. Her lack of shame. She might feel concerned about adultery and debt, but she wasn't ashamed.

Then I imagined Gemma, shameless – and me – between hotel sheets. Could this really happen? Was I destined to become her lover? Where would I take her? I began to sweat. I burned to see her, yet I was aghast, afraid. "Don't come," I implored her. "Stay away!" At the same time I urged her to hurry. Hurry!

12.15pm

12.30pm

12.45pm

At 12.55 it was quite plain that Gemma had stood me up. Over the past hour I had both dreaded and longed for her arrival and I suppose, logically, I should have felt both relief and disappointment at her non-appearance. Instead, I felt a pure rage.

Walking back to the old market, at almost every step I cursed – her youth, her body, her insouciance – and I cursed myself, for being a fool.

At the Rue Jeanne d'Arc a familiar roar made me glance to the left. There in the traffic was the red-and-white Volkswagen of Gemma Bovery. Instantly all was forgotten. She'd been delayed! It was a hot day, the circulation was bad, the city was crammed with tourists. Hardly her fault she was late. Once again, visions of us together swam in my head, the shared restaurant banquette, my thigh pressed hard against hers.

The van turned down a side street and I hurried after it, finding it a few minutes later, parked in the Place Pucelle d'Orléans.

There seemed to be a problem. Gemma was standing at the back, examining the engine.
I saw an opportunity to be of service and was about to make my presence known when a man got out of the passenger seat and joined her on the pavement.
I recognised him as the smart-arse friend of Madame Rankin – Patrick, the *anglais* with the excellent French.

Au Bois Chenu
Taverne de l'Moitre

Is it serious?
No..it always does this in traffic... ..overheats...

!

To my horror, he began to paw Gemma, and while at first she hunched and brushed him off like a wasp, she was soon giving him her full attention, putting both arms round his waist, while she gazed up at him . . .

We just have to wait!.. be **OK** when it cools down... **VW's** are **air-cooled**....

But ***I'm*** not, Gemma..

I left Gemma and Patrick still nuzzling on the pavement. If I'd stayed a second longer I would have done him some damage, I swear it – a good kicking *dans les tripes*. I walked aimlessly, too angry to feel like lunch. And as I walked, the letter I'd composed for Gemma, the one I'd sweated over for two evenings, crackled in my pocket. To hell with her! She'd have to write to the lawyer without my help and if Madame de Bressigny sued, serve her right.

Then for the second time that day I heard a familiar din – the belching racket of Gemma's Volkswagen as it came slowly down the street. As she went by she laughed at Patrick, her head close to his. She never glanced my way. This made me even angrier, made me want to thump the van, to yell an obscenity in the window.

I began to follow. Not too hard, given the van's sluggish pace.

It went down the the Rue Guillaume le Conquérant, and vanished. I saw it reappear at the Place Cauchoise, which it circled three times before going down the Rue Lecanuet. For some minutes it hesitated near the Musée des Beaux Arts and finally I caught sight of it disappearing down the underground parking at the Hotel de Ville.

I waited a few minutes. I was out of breath, but also I wanted to give them time to park and return to street level. I certainly didn't want to meet them. My plan was to jolt Gemma's memory – to find the van and to put my letter under her windscreen wiper.

P
Hôtel de Ville
GB
HDL
513E

SORTIE

I took the letter out of my pocket but, as I approached, a movement in the van startled me. A slight movement in the curtains, which had been drawn. The van itself seemed to rock gently, to thrum on its soft suspension.

Oh! la salope!

J'ai des envies de meurtre! Mais quelle salope! I could KILL her!!!

And with that curse I sealed Gemma Bovery's fate.

Menu

Dear Patrick

You may never read this. Earlier tonight, you asked me for the first time ever, what I was thinking. You didn't wait for my reply – you were busy showing off your French to the head waiter. I was thinking this: I really hate what happened yesterday in the van – not because it wasn't exciting and incredible – it WAS – that's the trouble. I hate it because I wasn't able to resist you. You always had that effect on me and you know it. For old Times' sake, you said. I was too pathetic and carried away to remember that old times weren't that great – 100% misery for me by the end.

I agreed to come out tonight because I couldn't help it, because I've had fantasies about you ever since we bust up. I wore this dress because I wanted to impress you. I thought everything would be different. Big mistake! Nothing's changed. You still talk at me; you walk behind me, smirking at other blokes – "Look what I'm knocking off!" I feel like a piece of your kit – like your watch or your bloody Mont Blanc pen. And I realise you're only interested in me because Pandora's kicked you out and you're feeling a bit spare. I've let you use me. You've often made me feel bad. I want this to be the last time.

..huîtres de St Vaast..et un caquelon de coquillages.... Madame, elle prend la Mosaique de Lotte et rouget au gingembre.. ...et pour moi le filet de boeuf...

..Course, you don't know about the restaurant I'm involved in... in Shadwell...**CREEL**..it's grown-up **Fish'n'chips'n'lobster**... Tim's designed it...***brilliant***...

...On dit parfois que la cuisine normande est un tantinet trop riche.... qu'elle baigne un peu dans la crême..Mais, c'est ça que j'aime: son côté solide, généreux, authenthique... en bref, c'est une cuisine du peuple

When I, Joubert, saw the heaving camper van in the Rouen car park, I was unaware that Patrick Large and Gemma had a history. I thought that they had only just met, not that he had once been the love of her life.
I ask myself, would knowing this have lessened my outrage? Would I have consoled myself that his previous relationship gave Patrick more right to be in the back of the van than me? And would it have been a comfort to learn that the passion they had rekindled was short-lived, that by the next evening Gemma wanted to extinguish it?

But why not, Gemma?..drive to your place...talk there...

Told you, I don't feel like it....
Why did you wear a dress like this then? mmh, you are so....

Patrick..look, I want to go..I want to be alone.... I'm in such a mess

What mess?
Oh, real mess ..I'm really in it

My husband seems to have left me...
..French lawyers are after me about an antique statuette..which I've lost
I owe a fortune The bank's frozen my account..,
My phone's cut off
Barclaycard's put their debt collecting outfit on to me...Amex won't be long

I used to earn quite a lot..so I had big credit limits..but I earn nothing much now... I just went on a mad SPEND...

Listen, Patrick, I'm going home now..out you get... Thanks for dinner...
Better kiss me goodnight, then

No..Patrick
Stop it

In the diary Gemma describes how she drove home, exultant and alone. She had resisted Patrick – an achievement which seemed to have given her the courage to confront everything that was wrong with her life. She did not go to bed. She sat at the kitchen table planning a course of action:
she would sell the house; she would ask Sannier for a valuation; she would face the bank and bargain for time to pay her creditors. Even though the house was more hers than Charlie's, she would split the proceeds with him, allowing him to clear his debts. She would see him right.
They still had a lease on the flat in London. She would return there and work like hell.
In the meantime she would empty the house and embrace a life of simple austerity.
A few floor cushions, yoga in the morning, everything a bit Zen. She would be THINGLESS.
She would cleanse herself mentally and physically, avoid alcohol and sex, and Patrick Large at all costs.

The following day Gemma went to Charlie's workshop to clear out some furniture that she had stored there – relics of her rustic phase that she thought might raise a little money.
There, standing behind the kettle and a box of teabags, was the missing statuette of Cupid and Psyche belonging to Madame de Bressigny.
The broken foot was in place, an invisible repair. Charlie must have mended it just before he left for England.

!!

..you mended it!... ..after I'd been such a shit to you... listen, I miss you, Charlie.....

Gemma Bovery called out to me in the lane. She reminded me of the letter I'd promised to draft to Madame de Bressigny's lawyer. It was a good thing, she said, I hadn't troubled to write it, because she'd just found the missing statuette. All that was needed now was a simple note informing Madame de Bressigny that she could collect her property whenever she liked. Would I, Gemma wondered, be very, very kind and help her write this in French?

I was speechless. I thought of the hours I'd spent composing her letter, of the way she had stood me up in Rouen – had stood me up for that *ordure*, that disgusting *anglais*, Patrick, all for a humping in the underground car park.

I turned my back, but I heard the gate open and then felt her hand on my shoulder. I don't know quite what she said. It was all so smooth, so cajoling, so caressing. Three minutes later I found myself in her house.

The salon was undergoing some re-arrangement, with the furniture piled at one end. The kitchen was in its usual state, the table covered with papers. Under a chair, bills, a half-eaten apple, a copy of *Madame Bovary*. A copy of *Madame Bovary*! The shock. I jumped backwards, as if it had been a landmine, knocking over a stool. I then froze. Gemma looked at me very strangely. Three times her gaze passed between me and the book. The book and me. Me and the book.

Oh my God...it was YOU, Raymond..wasn't it?

YOU sent me those pages from Madame Bovary, didn't you!?
You tried to ruin my thing with....

Oui, c'est vrai, mais...
YOU SOD!
How dare you!? How dare you interfere with my life!!?

One mineet!... I explain...

laisse-moi expliquer!
You spied on me! You bugger! You nosy bugger!

Enfin idiote! C'est pour ton bien que j'ai fait ça! For your good!
Ce livre! Ce livre! ...mais enfin...don't you understand the power of this book!??...
MADAME BOVARY

Don't you realise! Everyseeng wheech happen to Madame Bovary...happen to YOU!!!
Votre nom votre adultère.. your lovers! your debts!

At the end..she DIE! Elle meurt! SUICIDE!
!

Godsake! Don't spoil it! Don't tell me the END!.. haven't got that far!

Anyway, if you think I'm going to TOP myself over a few debts, you're MAD! BARKING MAD!!
Look...I want you to leave... Now! And leave me alone! ...Go on! Go away!
Mais Gemma, j'ai peur pour vous! Vous allez mourir...you weel die ... be careful...

"I want you to leave. Go away! Leave me alone."
These terrible words were the last Gemma Bovery ever spoke to me.

When I got home I began a letter of apology. I meant her no harm, I wrote. Far from it. Her well-being was of the utmost importance. I hadn't been so much spying on her as watching over her. The strange coincidences between her life and Madame Bovary's were, I hoped, just that – coincidences. When she had finished reading the book, she would surely come to understand my concern, my keeping a tender vigilance.

I took my copy of the novel to bed. As I imagined Gemma now doing, I turned to the final chapters and tried to read them through her eyes – the arsenic swallowing, Emma's horrible death, the funeral, Charles Bovary's demise.

There followed a night of hideous dreams. I was kneeling at the hem of a crinoline. A mountain of black silk towered above me. "Get up!" Gemma's voice called. As I rose, my eyes made a slow ascent of the skirt, over the hips, past the waist to the upper slope of the bodice with its dusting of snowy powder. "*L'arsenic,*" Gemma whispered as I fell.

I was in a misty place. Something grey, a figure, a Shade, pointed to a door. I became trapped in a small chamber, a sick-room, dark, hot, stale, and in the corner, someone sobbing, or gasping . . .

Gemma! Non! Non!

I woke to my own gasps, my own stifling bedroom, the oppressive August night. Outside, the mutterings of leaves, the thud of fruit falling from the trees. In my head the static whine of eternity.

I knew what I had to do.

Down in my study I prepared three envelopes. The first to Charlie Bovery in England. (His business card had his London address.) The second to the Rankins and the third, at the same address, to Patrick (I didn't know his surname then.)
You see, I had to sound an alarm. I felt very afraid for Gemma Bovery.
Something was closing in on her, something was going to happen to her.
I knew it. Self-destruction. Murder.
An accident of some sort.

The next day, after my duties at the bakery, I took my English translation of *Madame Bovary* and, as I'd done before, made photocopies of several pages. This time I chose Emma Bovary's suicide and the unpleasant details of her deathbed, and also one or two passages which mentioned debt (e.g. "I'm ruined, Rodolphe! You've got to lend me one hundred and forty pounds.") I divided the copies into three sets, sealed them in the envelopes and sent them off. Anonymously. Two would arrive the next day; Charlie's, in England, would take a bit longer.

It did occur to me that it wasn't perhaps the best time for the Rankins to receive this rather morbid despatch, overwhelmed as they were with preparation for Madame's birthday party. (The nightmare, she had told me, feeding turbans of fish to sixty people.)

But, I reasoned, no one is ever too busy to ignore a cry for help, are they?

'Course it's from her, Mark! God! Really! Honestly! How sick! How TACKY can you get!?
But what's it all about?

She's in shtuck!..it's all her own bloody fault Charlie did a bunk...she was shagging everyone - that Frog and now Patrick....

She spent too much on the house...now she's broke and feeling sorry..... Honestly! What a pain in the arse, sending this!!! It's really SICK!!

But Wizzy, what if this is for REAL? Gemma might really be, going to do a Madame Bovary....

What? Take arsenic? She'd better bloody not - she's doing my table decorations!

Look, I'll give her a ring. NO! I can't - her phone's cut off...ohh! Haven't time to go round there now...
I'll go, Wizzy.. I'll pop round... see if she's O.K.

Mark, I PROMISE! I didn't send you it... but I know exactly who DID - Joubert! ...the baker! He's bonkers.. I mean MAD! BARKING!!!

Because of my name and because I've got a bit of a cash-flow problem, he's convinced I'm going to kill myself...
But you aren't going to, are you?

Course not!
So... is it bad, the cash-flow problem?

Bad enough
Meaning?

25 grand will sort it. The interest and stuff.
£25,000?

That's nothing! Not a snorting great debt, is it?
It is to me

It's always interesting... The precise sum of people's misery...

Although you don't look too miserable, Gemma. You look GREAT...

I'm sure there's a way I could help...if you'd let me... Eh?

Oh, piss off, Mark ...get back in your basket.
Oops! Sorry! OK, OK..fine, fine! Sorry

No bones broken OK? See you, OK? Take care!

Now I come to something I've been dreading, the final entry in Gemma's diary, a dozen or so paragraphs written in a brisk, confident hand.

And then an eternity of empty pages.

Because they are her last lines, one demands more from them. I don't want to read the details of her *petit train-train quotidien*! I want to read something valedictory, an outpouring, a settling of accounts, a final adieu. But Gemma, unaware that her time is running out, writes at some length about the weather (the insufferable heat, the prospect of thunder). Next she dwells on her difficulties with the table decorations for Madame Rankin's party the following day (whether the French beans will stick to the pots properly, whether the sunflowers will remain upright).

There are problems, too, with her work – the drawing of the "wellies" (?) she has done for *Your Kitchen Garden* (two left feet) and the perspective of the greenhouse "totally up the creek."

After this there follow some observations about her main room which is now entirely cleared of furniture and looks "really cool, pared down to its architectural bones." She never wants to own a sofa again. She never wants any furniture higher than a floor cushion. At this point her writing is interrupted by Patrick Large, who had walked over from the Rankins' house.

God!

Have the bailiffs been already?
No! Just had a clear out Got fed up with all that tart's boudoir stuff...
If the bailiffs come, they're welcome to it.

Wanted something modern... clean... minimal...
Mm..looks great! ..I like it.

Patrick came over because he'd had one of Joubert's bloody envelopes too!! – the same as Mark and Wizzy. Does Joubert know about me and Patrick?! Patrick said I should get him for stalking and harassment – but really, it's not worth it, if I'm moving soon. Talked to P. about selling up and making deals with creditors. He said why didn't I declare myself bankrupt & be done with it? He said it was no big deal – everyone he knew went bust five years ago. They just take your passport away. He doesn't know what they do to you here in France. Then he asked where I planned to live when I got back to England.

I don't know... depends how things sort out with Charlie. But I think I'd want to be on my own – I seem to be better on my own – and I actually like it...
Gemma, you know what? I think you should come and live with me in London... Yeah?
I *mean* it... I've been thinking... the first time I knew you, I really ballsed it up, didn't I? I'm sorry. Thing is, the last few days made me realise: ***I really like you... I really want you to be with me...***
!
Come and live with me ... ***think about it***...
Patrick, it wouldn't work, I ***know*** it wouldn't. Things are different.. ***I'm*** different. It just wouldn't work.
Is it because you're afraid I'd dump you again?
Look, I wouldn't. I'm really serious about this...

I know more or less what Gemma did that evening. I know that Patrick Large left her around 6.30 because he passed my wife in the lane and commented, in exquisite French, on the heat. He was walking in the direction of the Rankins' *manoir*.

At 8.30 Gemma could be seen watering her plants.

An hour later the light was on in her bedroom. I assume it was then that she finished writing her account of the day – a day which had ended with the surprise of Patrick asking her to live with him. When she knew him in London this was something she had longed to do. She writes that if he'd asked her back then she would have yelled "Yes, yes!" But now she knows there are better things ahead than sharing life with Patrick and his giant ego. She is able to write decisively, "<u>I don't want to live with him</u>," and the pressure of her underlining shows on several of the empty pages that follow.

At 10.30, by my watch, Gemma extinguished her light.

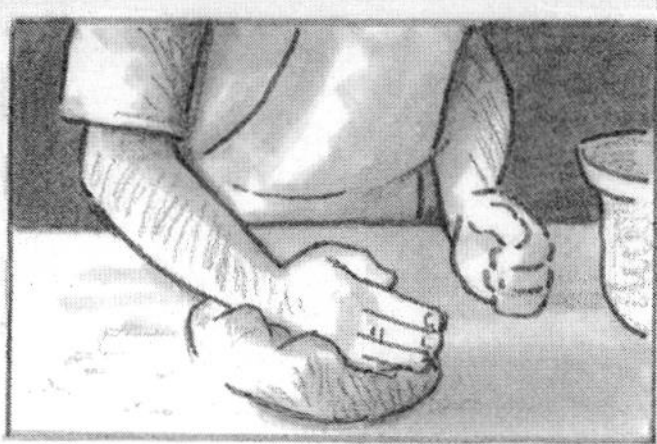

I, Joubert, spent another wretched night, sweating, wracked with guilt and unease. At 3.45 I was in the study rewriting my letter of apology to Gemma. An impossible thing. How does one excuse oneself for the deliberate invasion of someone's privacy? At 4.30, before daylight, I was dressed and on my way to the bakery, eager to work. For one thing we had extra bread to bake that day – the order for Madame Rankin's party – but also I needed the therapy of action, the comfort of routine, the feel of the dough springing under my fingers.

At midday I left the shop, earlier than usual, carrying one of my loaves still warm from the oven. It was a peace offering for Gemma, which I had decided to deliver with my letter before lunch.

As I opened Gemma's gate, I heard a sort of singing, a succession of strange undulating notes, which I recognised at once as the songs that whales sing to each other, those haunting motets of the ocean. The sounds came from a patch of shade where Gemma Bovery knelt with her back very straight (a posture once familiar to me as a preparation for *Pranayama*). "Ahh," she went three times. Then "Ooh," then "Mmm," then "Ohmm," all three times. I didn't dare disturb her. The door was open and I went in the house to the kitchen, where the dog Carrington lay panting in her basket, too hot to raise anything more than a little gruff snort. I placed the bread and the letter on the table. And then I left. Over my shoulder I saw Gemma still in a position of yogic calm, utterly at peace, while beside her the humpback whales continued their eerie carolling.

It was the last time I saw her alive.

We had got as far as the cheese, or rather I had – Martine never eats much at lunchtime. This was the first meal in weeks that I'd eaten with any sort of enjoyment. The sight of Gemma meditating in her garden had made me less anxious. Nothing bad, I thought, could happen to someone in such a state of yogic bliss.
I was broaching the Camembert when there was the sound of a vehicle which had turned into the lane and drew up near our entrance. Martine seemed strangely agitated. We both got up from the table to investigate.

Think it's Charlie! He's back from England!
Why's he stopped here?
!

Strange..leaving his van here......perhaps he wants to give Gemma a surprise

I'd never been so glad to see anyone as I was to see Charlie.
All is well now, I thought. And it's my doing. Charlie received my envelope and it's brought him back to Gemma. He'll look after her now. She's safe. All is well.

I settled down on the *canapé*.
I dreamed a cow was lowing in our garden, a sound which didn't stop when I opened my eyes. I looked at the clock. I had been asleep perhaps five or six minutes. The bellowing grew louder. I looked out of the window and saw a figure running across the field next to the house. Charlie Bovery. Charlie Bovery yelling. Charlie, with blood on his face.

Help! Joubert!
Joubert!... Help! Please! Telephone!
Gemma!..it's Gemma! She's **DEAD!** She's **dead!!**

Gemma dead! The disaster waiting to happen had happened. I'm ashamed of the way I reacted – as if it was my tragedy, not Charlie's – but I couldn't help it. I knew without being told that she'd done it like Madame Bovary, with rat poison, arsenic.

I knew it! Je le savais! Je le savais!

Elle a pris de l'arsenic!!? ...de la mort-aux-rats?
Joubert! for Godsake!..

Your phone! Let me phone the emergencies!
Elle est morte!

I was no use to Charlie. But my wife having heard the commotion shouted to him that she would ring for help. At this Charlie sprinted back across the field to his house.
I know I made it hard for Martine to explain on the phone. Several things had occurred to me. Was Gemma really dead? Because if she'd taken arsenic – and I was adamant in my crazed state that she had – its lethal effects took some time to work. Therefore she was still alive, *non*? But then wait, Charlie had blood on him. Gemma's blood? Had she shot herself? Was it the razor in the bath? Was the house awash with gore? Martine relayed none of this to the emergency service. She finished the call, and told me very calmly that she was going over to the Boverys' house.

Much of that dreadful afternoon has become lost in a blur. But some things are inscribed on my memory: the white heat as we ran over the field, the pounding of our feet on the dusty ground, the thudding of my heart, the rasping of my breath.
I remember, as we approached the house, hearing the ambulance arrive. Only it wasn't the ambulance yet, it was the crimson Peugeot of Madame de Bressigny. Madame de Bressigny, who I now assume must have come to collect her porcelain statuette. She asked us if Madame Bovary was in, and I replied, "Yes. But in no condition to see anybody." I felt bound to add that she was, in fact, dying. "Don't go in there," I told her. "It may be horrible. She's taken arsenic. It was her debts, *vous voyez, Madame*."

Madame de Bressigny looked at me as if I were an imbecile. Just then the ambulance arrived. She gasped, excused herself, and made for her car.
In the Boverys' kitchen a stool had been knocked over. That was the only sign of disturbance.

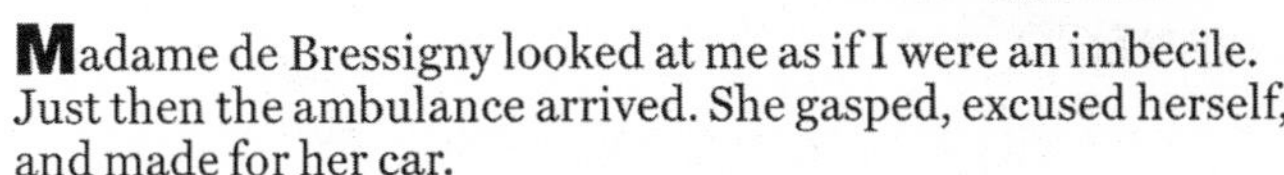
My letter of apology was not on the table,
but my peace offering of bread was there.
Part of a simple meal of salad and cheese.
A quarter or so of the loaf
had gone.

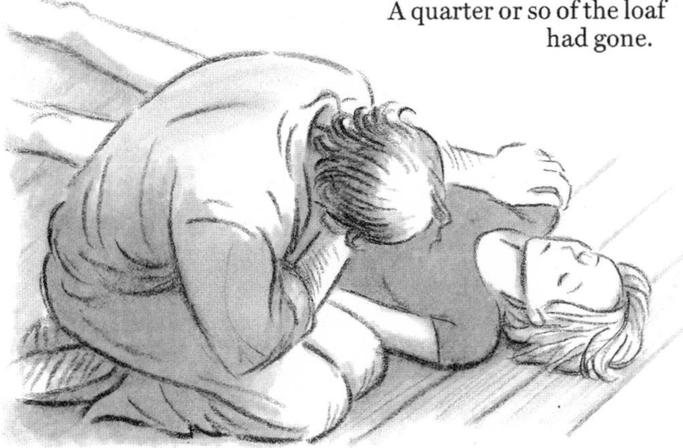

On the dresser was a blaze of yellow, the decorations Gemma had prepared for the Rankins' party – pots of sunflowers. Some of them seemed to turn their faces away from the scene on the floor where Charlie knelt beside his wife.
Gemma was quite grey.
She bore no sign of violence.
She was dead.
There was no question about that.

There was nothing the ambulance could do for Gemma. It had been gone a minute when a Range Rover arrived, bearing the Rankins and one of their guests who, they announced, was a doctor – a plastic surgeon. (How they heard about the tragedy is something which still puzzles me – with no telephone, it couldn't have been Charlie who told them.)

Omigod! Omigod!

..but Mark, we can't have the party! We have to cancel!!.
Can't cancel! It's too Late! People are on their way.

Wizzy Rankin had brought several bottles of whisky and a mobile phone. She went into the house and came out quite soon, dabbing her eyes. But after a few moments she took control, organising, opening the scotch, sitting Charlie down, helping him make calls to England and, with my wife's assistance, dealing with all the things which have to happen in such events – the visit of the *médecin légiste*, registering the death and so on.

AAihihaghihih!
Joubert!

As for me, I was a disgrace. I made a spectacle of myself, according to Martine. She thought I'd gone crazy. All I remember is standing in the garden, while Mark Rankin and his friend discussed the accident over and over again, as if repetition could give it some meaning, as if words could transform its awful banality. Every time those calm British voices mentioned the cause of death it was like a punch in my guts. I wailed. I couldn't help it. Gemma had choked, that's what the ambulance man said. And that's what Charlie told us in the kitchen, standing there with his broken glasses, a small blood-stain on his shirt. (But no sign of the blood I'd seen earlier on his face. Had I dreamed it?)

Gemma choked on a bit of bread. My bread! The bread I'd left on her table only three hours before. It was my bread that killed her. In other words, not only had I influenced the events of her life, but I had also been the instrument of her death. A dozen times the plastic surgeon tried to reassure me that I was in no way responsible, that it was a very common accident, something that could happen any time, to anyone. I wanted to kick him.
I was not responsible? Gemma's death, commonplace?

Do you understand my grief, my horror, my shame? Do you understand what kept me staring into the dark that night? A very black night – that is, until the early hours, when a series of explosions lit up the sky. It had been too late to cancel the Rankins' party. Someone must have decided, after all, to light the fireworks. "Is this what life is," I thought, as I watched the rockets, "a brief bid for the stars, a beautiful flash, a bang, and then a falling stick?"

Normandy

The Present Day

Gemma Bovery has been in the ground a few weeks, in the cemetery here in Bailleville.

PAIN MAISON
JE PETRIS ET JE CUIS MON PAIN AU FOURNIL
PAIN COMPLET
NAPOLEON

There is no headstone on the grave yet, but Wizzy Rankin tells me she will organise it – as she organised everything concerning Gemma's death and, so I've heard, paid for it too. Paid for the coffin, the flowers, the *pompes funèbres*, the cost of the burial and the refreshments afterwards at her house.

The Rankins are of course *richissimes,* but nevertheless, their generosity is impressive. Charlie Bovery, with all his financial troubles, couldn't have given Gemma any sort of funeral.

Martine and I went to the service, held in a chapel of rest in Bailleville. Some retired English priest said a few words and there were perhaps twenty other people: Gemma's stepmother, her half-brothers, a friend or two from England, the girl from Salon Nymphée who did Gemma's highlights, and astonishingly, in sunglasses and at the back, Patrick Large. Either Charlie didn't know Patrick had become Gemma's lover again, or perhaps he didn't care. Later at the Rankins' house I saw them talking together with perfect civility for several minutes.

Life continues. Thankfully, local interest in the accident has dwindled since it was in the newspaper. Customers no longer pump me for details. They no longer comment "Just like Madame Bovary!" and then contradict themselves: "*En fait*, not at all like her. Madame Bovary killed herself, whereas this *anglaise* choked on a croissant, *non*?"
How ignoble her death sounds. Even comic.

DRAME

Funeste coincidence

■ Une jeune femme a trouvé la mort hier à Bailleville. Gemma Bovary (31 ans) a été trouvé dans sa cuisine par son mari, gisant par terre après avoir avalé un croissant. Son voisin, le boulanger M. Raymond Joubert a porté secours, mais hélas, trop tard pour ranimer la jeune femme.

Charles et Emma Bovary, anglais tous les deux, vivaient à Bailleville depuis deux ans.

Tragic coincidence

■ A young woman died yesterday in Bailleville. Her husband found Gemma Bovary (31) lying on the floor of her kitchen having swallowed a croissant. Her neighbour, the baker Raymond Joubert, came to her aid but, unfortunately too late to save her.

Charles and Emma Bovary, both English, had been living in Bailleville for two years.

To me it is not comic. I don't eat and I can't sleep. I tell Martine it's my troubled colon, when really I want to unburden myself and tell her everything: about loving Gemma, watching her, stalking her, sending her anonymous mail and stealing her diaries. But I can't. Not yet. Not to Martine. And not to Charlie either. It sounds too squalid.
All the same, I feel an urgent need to talk to Charlie. Not to confess so much as to clear the air. That is why I find myself on a September afternoon walking across the field to Charlie Bovery with a bag containing his wife's diaries.

Ever since Gemma's death I have looked in on Charlie Bovery almost daily. Out of neighbourly concern, naturally, but also because I've been terrified that the curse of Madame Bovary hasn't run its course and that sooner or later I'll find him dead in the garden (the fate of Charles Bovary at the end of the novel).

But time has gone by and nothing has happened to Charlie. He drinks, and grieves, he works a little, he allows prospective buyers to look round his house. I should feel more relaxed about him. But I don't. I oscillate between feeling guilt over my part in his wife's death on one hand, and anger on the other. I am enraged at him for not behaving like a man, for choosing to ignore Gemma's lovers, for allowing it to happen.

Rage or guilt. Today I feel guilty.

When I arrive, Charlie's in the kitchen –the only room whose decor has survived from Gemma's rustic period. Usually he's pleased to see me.

Ah.. Raymond ..it's you. Come in.

I want to talk to you...I've wanted to talk to you for a long time
I'll get you a drink...

Today it's different. Charlie looks me in the eye for once. An accusing look. The look of a man determined to dredge up something nasty from a swamp. I feel terror. He's found out! He knows all my secrets.

OK, Charlie! O.K! I tell you...I tell you every theeng!

Je ne peux plus le supporter!

First: I steal...then I read ALL the intimate journals of of your wife...in this bag, here...

Second: I am GUILTY! Je suis coupable, Charlie!

Je suis coupable de la mort de Gemma!....in a certain way I KEEL her! Je l'ai tuée!!!

I keel her!! Ce n'est pas ce que je voulais...mais c'est passé! Je suis responsable de sa mort!
Raymond! Shut up, Shut up!

Stop! Please, please Raymond, don't talk balls... How could you have killed her? How could you be guilty?

It's ME that's guilty,.. I killed her, Raymond I killed Gemma!

Toi??
You keel your wife!? Tu l'as tuée??!!

But HOW?
How did you keel Gemma, Charlie?

It's what I wanted to talk to you about...

I can't bear it any longer! I have to tell someone!
Alors dis-moi

Charlie's account

"Well. I was pretty fed up with Gemma. Generally, because she never knew what she wanted and changed her mind all the time. And I was fed up because she'd had this affair with somebody local. Somebody in Bailleville. I knew all about it. She wasn't that discreet. It made me feel terrible. I was so jealous. But I never faced her with it because I knew it would blow over soon enough, and it did. Trouble was, when it did, she went on moping and living in another world. She didn't seem to need me. So I thought, 'sod it,' and went back to London, moved in with our lodger, slept on the sofa.

She started to wear perfume to walk the dog..she became slim and beautiful......
I followed her once... I saw her meet this bloke at the chateau...

"Then one day she rang me up and apologised for everything. Said she missed me. And the next day she put it all in a long letter. She said she loved me and she was going to get a grip on things, sell the house, and sort out our money problems and maybe we'd give it another go in London. Or somewhere.

just wanted to say I was sorry, that's all. I'm not asking to be forgiven

thing is, Charlie, I don't know what I want - only what I don't want.. except I would like to see you again

"**B**ut in the same post someone sent me all these pages from *Madame Bovary*, all about suicides and deathbeds. The postmark was Bailleville, but I knew it couldn't be from Gemma, it's just not like her. I don't know why, it really worried me. I thought, 'I'd better go back to Normandy and see how things are.' So I got the ferry from Dover, and all the way driving here I thought about Gemma. I was quite hopeful, you see. I thought we'd begin again.

"When I got to Bailleville, I stopped the van in the lane and walked up to the house. You see, I wanted to surprise her. It was a hot day and all the doors were open. I heard noises.

"A man's voice, panting. I went into the kitchen and there they were at it."

!

"I just went mad when I saw them. I didn't stop to think," Charlie told me. "I knew the bloke was English because he said my name. I just wanted to kill him, I was so angry. I mean, Gemma had written me all this stuff saying she was sorry for hurting me after her affair with the bloke in the chateau. And there she was having it away with somebody else! I was wild."

Leave my wife alone! You bastard! you bastard!
Stop! Charlie...
Stop! Charlie! Stop!
Listen!
Leave her ALONE!
You hear!
Listen! Charlie!
You bloody fool!
You bloody fool!
I realised who it was - I'd never met him, but I knew him... He was Gemma's boyfriend before she married **me**....
Patreek Large!

Charlie's account

"Patrick was yelling about Gemma, and it was then I realised that she was on the ground. Unconscious or dead, I didn't know. She was a weird colour. Patrick said she'd been choking and he'd been trying to do that thing you do for chokers – you hit them in the diaphragm. Only, he said he couldn't make it work.
When I came into the kitchen I thought he was doing something else."

That's what I mean, Raymond... **I KILLED** Gemma! If I hadn't started fighting, Patrick might have saved her....
Every second counted - it only takes a few minutes...to choke to death...

Charlie continues, "After that I ran to your house to telephone and Patrick rushed to the Rankins because they'd got a doctor staying.

The odd thing is, we hadn't made an agreement, but neither of us said anything about our fight to anybody.

Although it was probably obvious: Patrick had a black eye and my nose was bleeding.
No one asked us, so we said nothing, and after a bit it just didn't seem to matter.

It didn't change anything.
Gemma was dead and they'd taken her away.

The Rankins' party was that evening, but Patrick didn't feel like it. He came round here and we got drunk. He told me it was his fault she choked. He made her angry while she was having lunch."

But I've **told** you, Patrick! I just don't want to live with you

I don't love you...

But you did once, Gemma, didn't you?
Patrick! will you just
!?..

Charlie falls silent. I, Joubert, sit there. I'm thinking, *en fin de compte*, it really was an accident. No one's to blame – or only inadvertently: Charlie for fighting Patrick, Patrick for making Gemma choke on the sandwich and me, very, very remotely, for having given her the loaf.

Tears fill my eyes and I weep. For Gemma, for the waste of her life, and for Charlie, for his heart, which I think is broken. I reach behind me for a handkerchief. Is it by chance that my hand falls not on the box of Kleenex but on Gemma's copy of *Madame Bovary*?
At once I am terrified.

Aah!

What is it?! What's the matter?
Ce livre, Charlie!

Charlie! J'ai peur! Everytheeng in thees book, eet 'appened to Gemma! **Everytheeng!**... and eet weel 'appen to you!!
GUSTAVE FL
MADAME
BOVARY

Madame Bovary- she **DIE**!.. and then... Monsieur Charles Bovary... **HE DIE!!!**
Charlie! j'ai peur pour toi! ..tellement peur! Please! Don't **DIE**! Please!

What is all this, Raymond? I'm not thinking of **DYING**!
But Charlie! Charles Bovary – he **dies**!

Ah là là! Raymond! **ARRÊTE!**

Bonsoir, Charlie
Oh, Martine! You are kind to do all that
!

I am surprised, my wife walking into Charlie's house, with a pile of ironed clothes. How long has she been coming into his house without knocking? Since when has she been doing his laundry? Has she been doing anything else for him?

Martine reads my thoughts. She and Charlie, she says, are good friends. I, Joubert, might have noticed this, if I'd had time for anyone other than myself and *Madame Bovary*. This past year, she went on, I, Raymond, have been so boring to live with, so obsessed with that infernal book, muttering, talking in my sleep. *Madame Bovary* this, *Madame Bovary* that. Martine then turns to Charlie, "I suppose he's been telling you that you're going to die, like Charles Bovary? You're going to drop dead in the garden?"

Well, he has touched on it. Yes
Mais..

Mais Charlie...écoute... There is so much coincidence! So much!

First: you came here.... en Normandie..

And then, your **NAMES**! Just as the book!

Emma Bovary – your wife: Gemma Bovery! Charles Bovary – and you: Charlie Bovery.!
Raymond! ça suffit!
So boring!

But, listen, hang on a minute! My **real** name's not Charlie... or Charles..
Comment?

People call me Charlie, but it's not my real name... show you my passport if you like....

I was called after my grand father..

Cyril

Cyril?? **Cyril Bovery**?
Yes. Does that change anything?

Ah, Cyril! Quel bonheur!

Epilogue

It's spring, and the Boverys' apple trees are in blossom. A few months ago Charlie – or Cyril, as I now try to think of him – sold the house at a price which, according to Madame Rankin, more or less paid off his debts, and those of Gemma.

Charlie lives in London now, in the same rented flat. He has his children nearby, and his workshop, and (again according to Madame Rankin) a girl-friend, a solicitor he met on the ferry.

When he left here he promised to come back and visit, but I doubt he will. Bailleville holds too much sadness for him. That's why he left the dog, Carrington, behind. He gave her to us, he said he couldn't bear her mournful look. So now Carrington is mine, and looks at me from time to time with an infinite sadness.

But every so often something sends her crazy with joy. When she hears the roar of Gemma's camper van, for example. (Charlie was obliged to sell it. The Rankins gave him a good price – another classic vehicle to add to Mark's collection.)

And if I walk with Carrington near La Boissière, I have to remember to keep her on a lead or she's off like a greyhound, barking at the side door of the chateau, where she must have spent many pleasant afternoons dozing in the hall while Gemma was in the salon with Hervé. And sometimes, I know, she was indulged with titbits of the lovers' snacks.

As for Hervé, he wasn't seen in Bailleville all last summer. One heard gossip, that he'd passed his law exams and that, after she'd discovered his affair with Gemma his girl-friend, Delphine, gave him the push. I saw him once, in November, in the cemetery. It was All Saints, and the Bressignys were there, putting flowers on the family graves, as were most of Bailleville. I watched Hervé walk over to the newer graves, where Gemma, Madame Bovery, lies.

As I said, it's spring now, and the Boverys' apple trees are in blossom. There's a furniture van outside the house: the new owners are moving in. They're English too, like the Boverys. A couple. He's older than her, Martine tells me. She met the wife in the lane. Her name is Jane. Jane Eyre.